PADDLING

through TIME

PADDLING *through* TIME

A Sea Kayaking Journey through Clayoquot Sound

Joanna Streetly

Photography by Adrian Dorst

RAINCOAST BOOKS

VANCOUVER

First published in 2000 by

Raincoast Books
8680 Cambie Street
Vancouver, B.C.
V6P 6M9
(604) 323-7100
www.raincoast.com

1 2 3 4 5 6 7 8 9 10

CANADIAN CATALOGUING IN PUBLICATION DATA

Streetly, Joanna.
   Paddling through time
   (Raincoast journeys)

   ISBN 1-55-192-278-9

   1. Clayoquot Sound Region (B.C.)   2. Clayoquot Sound Region (B.C.) – Pictorial works.
I. Dorst, Adrian. II. Title.
FC3845.C53S77 2000   971.12   C00-910135-7
F1089.V3S84 2000

Editing by Theresa Best
Cover design by Ruth Linka
Interior book design and typesetting by Val Speidel
Colour separations by DPI, Vancovuer
Printed and bound in Hong Kong, China

*Raincoast Books gratefully acknowledges the support of the Government of Canada, through the Book Publishing Industry
Development Program, the Canada Council and the Department of Canadian Heritage. We also
acknowledge the assistance of the Province of British Columbia, through the British Columbia Arts Council.*

To my father, John Streetly, in the spirit of adventure.

Contents

PAGE II–III *Sunset and moonrise: dusk near Kutcous Point. Once in a lunar cycle, the setting sun descends while the full moon rises. At times like this, it is hard to know whether to look east or west.*

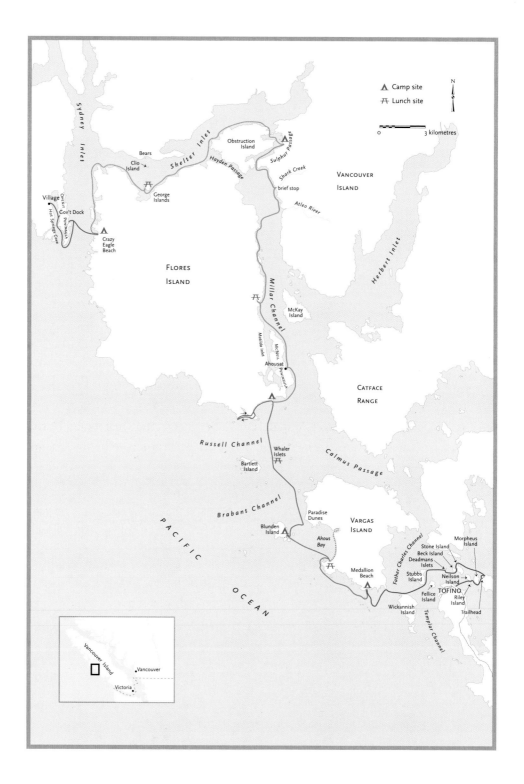

0   3 kilometres

Sydney Inlet

Bears
Clio
Island

Shelter Inlet

Obstruction
Island

Hayden Passage

Sulphur Passage

Shark Creek

VANCOUVER

ISLAND

brief stop

Atleo River

Village

Openit Peninsula

Gov't Dock

Hot Springs Cove

George
Islands

Crazy
Eagle
Beach

FLORES

ISLAND

Millar Channel

McKay
Island

Herbert Inlet

Matilda Inlet

McNutt Peninsula

Ahousat

CATFACE

RANGE

Russell Channel

Whaler
Islets

Bartlett
Island

Calmus Passage

Brabant Channel

Paradise
Dunes

VARGAS
ISLAND

PACIFIC

Blunden
Island

Ahous
Bay

Father Charles Channel

Stone Island
Beck Island
Deadmans
Islets

Morpheus
Island

Medallion
Beach

Stubbs
Island

Neilson
Island

TOFINO

OCEAN

Wickannish
Island

Fellice
Island

Riley
Island

Trailhead

Templar Channel

Vancouver Island

Vancouver

Victoria

Acknowledgements

WAS IT REALLY ONLY ONE YEAR AGO THAT I CATEGORICALLY DECLARED, "OH, I could *never* write a book"? And then, was it really only nine months later that I found myself saying, "That was exhausting. And I will *never* be able to write another one"?

Well, it wasn't really my doing. A host of people breathed life into this project, until it took on a life of its own and took charge of many things – me included.

Most importantly, I would like to express my respect for the Tla-o-qui-aht, Ahousaht and Hesquiaht First Nations, whose traditional lands have been such a source of inspiration to so many people, and to me personally, both as a writer and as a coastal resident.

Without the confidence and advice given to me by Dorothy Baert and Adrienne Mason, I would probably still be floating along in the I-could-never-write-a-book category. The Clayoquot Writers Group bolstered me up, too. And what would I have done without Janice Lore, Adrienne Mason and Andrew Struthers to be my second set of eyes, when all I could see was a haze of squiggles dimly revolving in the grey glow of the computer?

Then there are the Raincoast eyes: the eyes of Carol Watterson, Brian Scrivener, Derek Fairbridge, Theresa Best and the rest of the crew who have a better view of things than I, and who have chiselled this material into shape.

Much of the Native history in this book has been gleaned from within the pages of *Cultural Heritage Background Study for Clayoquot Sound* by Ian R. Wilson, E. Jane Warner, Nicholas I. Heap, Randy Bouchard and Dorothy Kennedy; but other people have shared valuable information, including Robert Martin Sr., Barry Campbell, Ken and Dot Gibson.

Joe Matuska of Aquabound provided the most beautiful paddle for this expedition – one of the lightest I have ever lifted. And Spike, from Necky Kayaks, offered the use of a kayak, which I just couldn't collect in time.

And then there are my friends: Jackie Windh, for her support, despite difficult circumstances; Cindi Cowie, for her invaluable role as the temporary manager of my life; Jan Brubacher, for paddling with me – and everything else.

Finally to my canine companion, Sweetheart, whose long sighs echoed down the hallways of my conscience every time I hunkered down for another stint at the computer. They still echo . . .

Foreword

There is nothing – absolutely nothing – half so much worth doing as simply messing about in boats.

—Kenneth Grahame, *The Wind in the Willows*

I LIKE TO THINK THAT MY CHILDHOOD LESSONS WERE TAKEN WITH DUE seriousness: that I learned them well and carried them with me into adulthood. And since I also like to ascribe a sense of worth to personal achievements, I valiantly endeavour to mess around in boats twice a day, at least.

In the chapters that follow, two friends and I immerse ourselves in boating for a solid week. The boats that we mess around in are sea kayaks, but on the ocean – in kayaks or in any other craft – the phrase "messing around" should not be spoken lightly. Respect for the ocean, skill and experience are prerequisites for any journey. Many years as a sea kayaking guide have embedded these principles deeply.

My first sea kayaking trip – two weeks on Vancouver Island's west coast when I was 18 – changed the course of my life dramatically. The feeling of wildness was something I couldn't shake, after living in England. I was hooked; I wanted more of it. The teenage quandary of what to do with my life was miraculously resolved: I would leave England and study outdoor recreation and wilderness leadership in British Columbia.

My new lifestyle led me back to the West Coast and, from there, into a career as a sea kayaking guide. The dose of magic from my first kayak trip had been potent, and its effects on my fate were long-lasting. Returning was inevitable, even if it hadn't been something I actually planned. But the "west coast of Vancouver Island" is a broad designation. Arriving in Tofino was a fluke – a lucky one. Suddenly, I had access to a coastal indent crammed with islands and inlets, beaches and mountains sheathed in virgin temperate rainforest. Clayoquot Sound is a kayaker's dream. Of the areas I have paddled, few can rival its beauty and intensity. I could hardly have landed in more exquisite surroundings. Not only that, my job took me outdoors daily. Over time, each nook of coastline acquired special significance; every place had an experience associated with it.

During the last three years I have worked at a local magazine and have guided fewer kayak trips. My time on the water has become more limited (and therefore more precious), despite living on a floathouse and travelling to town daily by boat. But the more I explore these waters, the more they beckon; commuting can count only partially as exploration. Exploration involves surrender − physical as well as mental − and this surrender requires time: days, preferably weeks.

On this particular surrender I am accompanied by Adrian Dorst, a photographer who is equally bewitched by Clayoquot Sound. He has lived in Tofino for decades and is a veteran explorer of these waters. Also on this journey is Jan Brubacher, my close friend and co-editor. Together we have sought sanctuary in Clayoquot Sound

Tofino (right) and Meares Island (left) emerge from the soft haze lingering over the waters of Browning Passage. Low cloud conditions are common here, and many a visitor to Tofino has come and gone without even knowing that Meares Island exists.

on many previous occasions – paddling away from our obligations with glee, seeking our inspiration at the source.

Last year the three of us were thwarted in our plan to have an adventure in the sound by the onset of bad weather. One year later, having almost grown webbed feet during the miserable winter and spring, we are desperate to get away. Our intent is to spend seven days meandering in a northwesterly fashion through Clayoquot Sound to Hotsprings Cove, 32 nautical miles as the crow flies from Tofino (many more nautical miles along the route we plan to take), to the bubbling, geothermally heated hot springs at Sharp Point.

We are venturing into a confluence of land and water, where islands, inlets, mountains, rivers and beaches swirl in myriad shapes against a Pacific horizon. A place of beauty and a place of harshness; it can be inviting and it can be unforgiving; it is a place of many histories and a place of many contradictions.

Fragments of this place exist within the pages of this book: a mish-mash of the past and the present, humans and animals, travellers and landscapes. For Clayoquot Sound cannot be singly described. Like a beach, it reveals a different bounty at every tide, drawing you back for more, inescapably, providing the perfect opportunity to immerse yourself in something extremely worthwhile: messing around in boats.

Chapter One
INTO THE GREEN

From Tofino, via Meares Island,
to Medallion Beach, Vargas Island

IT HAS BEEN A GRIM YEAR FOR WEATHER. LA NIÑA HAS BLOWN and rained her chilly way into our bones. It's now July 3, and just as we are embarking on a seven-day kayaking adventure, Adrian spots the first western sandpipers going south on their fall migration. Our spirits, already lowered by weeks of cold grey drizzle, sag visibly. But we launch the boats anyway, their waterlines perilously low with the week's cargo, and are sent off by several horn blasts from a friendly whale-watching boat.

If nothing else, it is good to be leaving Tofino. Situated at the tip of the Esowista Peninsula, Tofino seems charming and peaceful, but the serenity of the inlets and islands of Clayoquot Sound, sitting so calmly on one side, is counterbalanced by the crash of the Pacific on the other. The village is sandwiched between conflicting physical energies, and to some extent this is reflected in the human character of the town. A recent census estimates that there are 1,170 people living here, with one of the highest voter turnouts in the country.

The trunk of the hanging garden tree is trimmed with the fibrous bark characteristic of western red cedars. Nuu-chah-nulth people collected this bark for clothing, ropes and basketry without causing lasting damage to the tree. The practice of bark gathering is still alive today.

The Tla-o-qui-aht, whose traditional lands Tofino occupies, called this site Nu-chucks ("looking out over everything") and used it for just that purpose – as a lookout – before it became inhabited by Europeans in the late 1800s. The peninsula was used as a lookout of a different sort when an airbase was set up at Long Beach during World War II, at times stationing as many as 4,000 men. Canada was determined to prevent these expansive beaches from acting as airstrips for The Enemy.

Twenty years later the wartime community was doused with Peace, as disciples of the sixties arrived, as if to Mecca, and took to living on the beaches. A unique lifestyle blossomed until Pacific Rim National Park arrived in 1970 and expropriated the land. Everyone was asked to leave, but many people continued to live in the surrounding area and still do, to this day.

Perhaps the first stirring of environmental protest came in 1984 with the proposed logging of Meares Island. Although one clearcut already existed on Meares, the idea of large-scale logging, as intended by MacMillan Bloedel, a logging company operating in the area, was horrifying to many people. When the Tla-o-qui-aht people declared Meares Island a tribal park and denied MacMillan Bloedel access to it, they were joined and supported by many people from Tofino in the first of several grassroots environmental actions.

After Meares there were civil protests at Sulphur Passage and Bulson Creek, and in 1993 there were spectacular blockades in Clayoquot Sound, where nearly 900 people were arrested for trying to save the area from chainsaws. In a small town, civil actions such as these have a great impact on residents. Overnight, home can become an armed camp, with everyone taking sides. And while challenging the status quo is important, it can also be divisive. In Tofino, divisions have been conspicuous for the last 20 years at least. However, local people have maintained a consistent dialogue with one another – heated though it may sometimes be – in an effort to find solutions, and many compromises have been made. Tourism has flourished, gradually replacing commercial logging and fishing with guest accommodations, whale-watching tours, sport fishing, sea kayaking and other recreational activities. But tourism is not without problems. Tourist-related businesses may provide financial opportunities, but filling a town of little more than 1,000 residents with half a million tourists each year inevitably challenges one's understanding of "home."

Right now we are in the throes of the Canada Day long weekend. This quiet, cloudy morning is a pleasant respite from the crowd-filled streets, and the prospect of a week out in the sound beckons delightfully. As we head over to Meares Island our mood lightens, despite the weather.

The fact of tourism is not likely to desert us on this trip, however. Fifteen minutes after leaving shore, we shoot out across the rapidly flooding current between Neilson and Morpheus Islands and rest in a back eddy behind a rock. On either side of us, the tide is running at three or four knots. Given that most kayaks travel between two and four knots, this current can significantly affect one's feelings about kayaking. If we had chosen to go against the tide this morning, we would be paddling like fiends right now and probably going backwards. But situated as we are, the current is not touching us. Under my hands are green sea anemones and an abundance of rockweed, its khaki-coloured bladders vibrant in the clear water. Either side of us the water skirls by – impossible to focus on – *in moto perpetuo*.

Mesmerized as we are, the sudden presence of a whale-watching Zodiac jars us cruelly. Rounding a corner at full blast, the vessel would have annihilated us had it

The sublime green slopes of Mount Colnett on Meares Island cushion this eagle's-eye view of Tofino's waterfront. Tofino's entire water supply comes from a handful of small creeks rushing down through the rainforest. The water is collected on Meares Island before being piped to a tank in Tofino.

arrived three minutes earlier. The boat speeds into the channel, does a U-turn around the rocks and flies past again, leaving us with mouths agape, as it skitters into Browning Passage to pull S-turns in front of another whale-watching vessel. My suspicions about the inverse relationship between horsepower and intelligence seem well founded.

During a small craft masters program, I learned that boats that are under power must give way to nonpowered boats. In real life, I have learned that – in Clayoquot Sound anyway – this is possibly the most disregarded of marine rules. My focus when kayaking here is to choose the route least travelled, to minimize any crossing of boat lanes and to travel with the presumption that I have not been seen.

Fortunately, away from the harbour area, boat traffic is much reduced. But it always pays to be aware of it, a fact of which we have just been well reminded. We look both ways before nosing out into the current once more, and ferry across to the shallow water near Morpheus Island, where we are safe from Pacific cowboys and their metal-rubber steeds.

Here, there is quietness, punctuated only by the clack of clamshells hitting rock, dropped by a determined crow. Once a cemetery for settlers, Morpheus Island is now municipally protected and lush with rainforest growth. It acts as one more barrier between us and the noise that inevitably travels across the water from Tofino. Paddling north along the shoreline, we find ourselves just across the channel from Meares Island. A cluster of kayaks announces the entrance to Big Tree Trail. We decide to paddle on to another, less-crowded landing.

The tide is running quickly in the little passageway created by a nearby islet. Over the shallows, the water glows a pale green, suddenly becoming dark and lugubrious as the rocky ledge drops deeply away. On the point ahead, as I look at Lemmens Inlet, a cedar curves gracefully out over the water. This spot has always been a favourite of mine, even before I discovered that it had once been the site of a traditional fish trap. Little trace of the trap remains now, most of it having been destroyed when Tofino's waterline was put in place. But as I slip through, I like to conjure images of Tla-o-qui-aht people setting up piles of rocks and branches at either entrance to the passage and waiting for the tide to ebb before collecting their catch. It's easy to travel these waters without realizing what an important source of seafood they were to the thousands of Native people who lived here, in the days before freezers and supermarkets. Two hundred years ago, we would have journeyed

Calm water near Meares Island makes for easy paddling. Headwinds can be the kayaker's greatest foe, making even short trips exhausting, forcing paddlers to choose the most sheltered – often the most circuitous – routes.

In the presence of the ancients: it can be fun to guess the age of a tree and imagine how it may have looked centuries ago. Here, the hanging garden tree on Meares Island may be as much as 1,500 years old.

without this quantity of packaged food; we would have expected to feed on bounty caught or found along our way. We might even have stopped right here at this fish trap, hoping for a few small perch to keep us going.

As it is, we keep going, paddling along the edge of the Arakun mudflats, with Lemmens Inlet stretching away from us – an alluring arrangement of water and tiny islands with velvety folds of rainforested mountains sloping down on either side. Moments later we glide into our landing site, surrounded on all sides by greenness. The water is dark and swampy; the hemlocks have sprouted lime green tips; the cedar and alder are a heavy green – in sharp contrast to the outrageously bright algae draped along the high-tide line. We stow our gear, tie our bowlines and head into the forest, into the green.

Walking the Big Tree trail on Meares Island is a bit like making a pilgrimage. At the time of the protest over Meares, one of the trees here was considered the largest cedar in Canada. It was an important find. The size of the tree somehow amplified the value of preserving the island. Its grandeur was exaggerated by the variety of life forms growing on it and it gradually became known as the "hanging garden tree." A trail was built and posters were made. Meares Island became visible to the public and support began to grow. The boardwalk along which our feet gently clump is a recent addition to this trail, but it follows the route that was established at the time of the protest. The route became so popular that the level of traffic, combined with the dampness, led to a serious problem with mud – the trail became lost in a morass of puddles; sometimes even gumboots were not enough protection for walkers; the forest floor became damaged; and in places the fragile habitat of animals such as salamanders was destroyed.

By 1992 some of the boat owners who had been taking people to Meares voluntarily gave up their business in favour of letting the trail recover. The trail was unused for two years. At the same time the possibility of building a boardwalk was explored. In the end a mixed crew of Tla-o-qui-aht and Tofino workers constructed this section of boardwalk, with financing from the Western Canada Wilderness Committee. But the boardwalk only covers the most travelled section of the trail – from the shoreline starting point to the hanging garden tree, an easy 20-minute walk. The rest of the trail forms a loop – about an hour and a half's walk before returning to the starting point.

Along the fringes of boardwalk, the deer fern fiddleheads are still partially curled – a sign of the lateness of the year; the salmonberries, too, are still out and plump – another indication of the cool summer, one that we are not complaining about, however.

Everything about this part of Meares suggests abundance, from the massive girths of the hanging garden tree and other western red cedars to the plump clusters of huckleberries and salal berries, just waiting to ripen. It's hard to believe that this forest is old, even though evidence of decay is everywhere. Vibrant colours and textures conceal the infinite processes at work here, but looking carefully, it is possible to see beyond the façade of colour.

The first challenge lies in attempting to feel the centuries of life these big cedars have experienced. Some of them may be a thousand years old or more, which brings us back to the 10th century. The forest may have looked remarkably similar then; it is said to have been evolving continuously since the glaciers started retreating 10,000 years ago. Coastal forests also have the distinction of being too moist to be significantly affected by fire. This environment, then, has experienced a long and continuous evolution, and may contain many invisible links to its ancient beginnings.

As I walk past an overturned cedar, I can see just how little of the tree was underground: it has a fantastic mosaic of roots swirling around, still tenaciously grasping rocks as if somehow there might be a chance for resurrection. These roots probably went down only two feet into the topsoil. The trunk itself is huge. Fallen over as it is, it still lies higher than my upstretched hand. Along the top of it several large hemlocks have grown, while piles of moss drape over – sagging, seeping, creeping down. And as my gaze falls downwards, the original wood of the tree becomes visible, crumbling and red, turning into topsoil before my eyes.

This is the way of the forest. If organic matter can find a place to lodge and accumulate, it will do so, decaying and producing soil in the process. Hence the so-called hanging garden trees with the microenvironments that develop in their gnarled, spired tops. If an organism can no longer cling to life, then some form of life will doubtless cling to it, and take from the organism any life it can. In this way, the existence of the rainforest is bound up in an extraordinary tangle.

Comprehending the interplay between the canopy and the forest floor is another challenge. Clayoquot Sound receives approximately 13 feet of rain a year. The earth in this forest is protected from the full force of that rain by the filtering effect of branches, needles and roots. This same system retains moisture, releasing it slowly throughout the year like a giant sponge. A blanket of moisture, in droplet and vapour form, exists between roots and canopy, dependent on both. Other species in the forest depend on this moisture as well, and have evolved complex relationships based on this environment over thousands of years. It is almost impossible to think of this spot being stripped of its trees – the overwhelming completeness of the ecosystem prevents it. At this moment, as I gaze around, I wonder about the struggle that would ensue if, once more, Meares Island became subject to logging.

Interestingly, this spot is not where the protest occurred. The action in 1984 took place at Cis-a-qis, also known as Heelboom Bay, on the east side of Meares. This bay was intended by MacMillan Bloedel to be a log sorting or boom area. Response from some of the Tla-o-qui-aht was swift. With help from Tofino locals they constructed a cabin at the head of the bay, and started carving three dugout canoes as a demonstration of their traditional use of the forest. It was also hoped that the sale of these canoes would help to raise money to save the island. Soon Meares Island was declared a tribal park. When MacMillan Bloedel tried to conduct their first day's work, Moses Martin, the elected chief of the Tla-o-qui-aht, greeted the forestry workers, welcoming them to their garden, but requesting them to leave their chainsaws in the boat.

Eventually, a moratorium on logging on Meares Island was declared, creating a stalemate. Since then, the Tla-o-qui-aht have twice attempted to take Meares Island through the courts as a land rights issue, both times without resolution, although the moratorium still holds. Even now, as the Tla-o-qui-aht people seek to reclaim land rights from the government, the issue of Meares is a grey area.

The island itself has two other features that worked in its favour during the protests: the sublime green slopes of Lone Cone mountain and Mount Colnett. They provide an irreplaceable backdrop to the village of Tofino. One only has to drive to nearby Ucluelet to see what it's like to live in the shadow of a clearcut. With Pacific Rim National Park being gazetted, those who were aware of the possibilities of tourism knew that scenery was an important lure. Also, the same green slopes provide Tofino's water. The current method of getting water is to tap into several of the small creeks that come down from Mount Colnett. Without trees to retain moisture, this source would dry up. Amazingly, these creeks manage to provide water for the huge number of annual visitors – and all the bathing and laundering that comes with them.

Right now we are at the foot of Mount Colnett; we have gone beyond the end of the boardwalk, with the intention of completing the loop. There are beautiful cedars everywhere, their crooked tops beckoning us on. The moss and the salal are thick and, in places, the mud is deep. Once in a while we come across Sitka spruce, with their magnificently straight trunks and their fantastic horizontal limbs, at least a hundred feet above us, so heavy with moss and ferns. It's easy to see the allure these delightful boughs have for birds such as the marbled murrelet. The murrelet, a pelagic bird, is renowned for its secretive nesting habits; only a few nests have ever been found. The birds fly into the forest after dark and leave before dawn, frustrating researchers who hear them but are unable to locate the nests. The few nests found have been little more than depressions in the moss. Clearcutting threatens these birds:

Draped with moss and lichens, the branches of a Sitka spruce reach through the forest canopy.
Branches like these may conceal the secretive, much-searched-for nesting sites of the marbled murrelet.

it takes years for these trees to grow to their average height of 200 feet with these horizontal limbs, and years for the moss to become as thick as pillows. For a bird that only comes to land for nesting purposes, it is important that the habitat be in place when they arrive; delay can make the difference between breeding successfully or not. To discover that their nesting areas have been destroyed is devastating to the murrelets. Fortunately this hasn't happened here on Meares. These branches are so far above us that we can hardly see them clearly, but it's still fun to think of the tiny chicks hiding amidst the moss and licorice ferns.

Given the intact appearance of this forest, it is easy to presume that it has never been altered by humans. It hasn't been clearcut — the method that leaves the most obvious evidence of human presence — so it is difficult to grasp how much it may have been used by First Nations people. They seem to have left no trace of their labours. There are clues, though. It is just that they are so subtle. We have walked past many trees that have been used but been left standing, having had only a section of bark or wood removed, but the work was done so discreetly the result is almost invisible. Wood taken from a living tree never exceeded a certain amount, so the ability of the tree to heal itself was not compromised. On many trees the scars blend into the naturally convoluted shapes of the trees. In other places, there is a mossy stump, cleanly cut, but no evidence of the accompanying tree trunk, which may have been removed to begin life anew as a dugout canoe.

Information gleaned from Europeans who passed by this area in 1835 suggests that Clayoquot Sound may have been home to 2,000 people at that time. These people were dependent on the cedar for nearly every aspect of their lives: the bark was used for clothing, weaving and rope making; planks they cut from it were used for longhouses; the trunks were used for canoes and totem poles. The cedar provided warmth and shelter; it allowed cultural development through art; it provided the means to hunt and fish; it facilitated travel and trade and thus a knowledge of other cultures. The identity of the people was enormously tied to the cedar. It was a magnificent resource, one that was respected and well used, but never "used" in a way consistent with any Western understanding of that word.

My wonder at this forest never ceases when I think of it as the historical showcase that it is. Museums are hardly necessary on this coast; all that is needed are eyes to look with and time for contemplation. And what better place for contemplation?

We have come close to the water again now and the forest has opened into a more visible stand of trees, brighter, with more of a feeling of space. In one place a magnificent cedar has fallen down the slope and steps have been cut into it. It's a definite stairway and a definite invitation to climb. Above it stands another cedar, wildly spiralled, twirling skyward like a twister.

Shortly before we regain the boardwalk, we come across a cedar that surely rivals the hanging garden cedar in its size, only this tree is clearly alive and healthy all over. The same cannot be said for the hanging garden cedar. The hanging garden cedar suffers from a peculiar problem: people have been so fascinated by it, so impressed and delighted, that they have climbed all over it, trampling the delicate soil and ferns at its base, eroding the already-receding bark and even – in some places – crawling through it, opening up the hole in the middle of the tree, exposing its secret centre. In short, the traffic of human visitors to the hanging garden tree has taken its toll. This rival cedar has not had the same fate. Yet. Its bark is heavy and rough, in places like a giant braid. Further up, a line of sapsucker holes accentuates its massive girth.

Finally we regain the boardwalk, the muffled noise of our feet pulsing out into the forest. Near our landing site, the boardwalk crosses a tiny creek that seems to emerge from under the roots of a cedar. It is a pretty spot, the water a focal point that draws the eye. But peer further into the picture, into the pool by the bridge, and it is possible to spot several large egg masses produced by the northwestern salamander. These shy creatures are one of the silent victims of clearcutting. Their secret life is largely invisible to humans; catching a glimpse of one is an exciting and rare event. Their need for moist, dark places links them irrevocably to the rainforest. They cannot compromise. Looking at these egg masses – so preposterously large compared to the salamander's tiny size – I think of the human practice of birth control. Children are so likely to survive these days, it is impossible to think of needing this quantity of young, just to ensure the continuation of the species.

The tide has receded while we have been walking. The boulders that we paddled over are visible now. It's time to go. To reach this spot, we crossed part of a huge shallow area that reaches into Lemmens Inlet. At low tide, the Arakun mudflats extend as far as the eye can see, forming one of several areas that make Clayoquot Sound an important stopover for migrating birds. These areas have been granted protection from activities such as dredging, but hunting is still allowed. In the spring and fall, flocks of birds continually arrive and leave, taking the vital nourishment they need to continue on their journeys. It is a birdwatcher's paradise. But to human beings, with loaded kayaks, this area is much more appealing when it is covered with water. We quickly bolt down some lunch – the idea of dragging the boats across miles of soft mud and eelgrass encouraging us to launch right away – and paddle fast.

We leave Meares to the sound of an avian riot: the crows are besieging a raven. This is the time of year when nests are pillaged and baby birds are very vulnerable. Despite the raucous clamour of the crows, we hear the raven once or twice, sounding smug, perhaps victorious. There is a bit of light in the west and still no wind. It is completely calm as we wind our way through the Tofino harbour islands, continuing on our journey.

West of the trailhead by about half an hour, at Deadman's Island, the resident eagles are at home, minding their nest. I feel connected to these birds because I have watched them build this nest from scratch, watched their babies grow and learn to fly, watched them huddle together in companionable gloom as the winter storms have pelted them with rain and wind. These birds have built their home in a conspicuous

Like silent gatekeepers, the Arakun Islands guard the entrance to Lemmens Inlet, Meares Island. The land at the far end is low lying, giving the false impression that the inlet continues on into Bedwell Sound (behind). For this reason it was originally referred to as Deception Inlet.

location, right next to a constricted boat lane. They are possibly the world's most viewed pair of wild eagles. Every boat tour in the sound includes a stop here and millions of eyes, including mine, have squinted up at them. I am pleased to see two tiny heads poking up over the debris of the nest. This pair seems to have remarkable success with their breeding, often raising two babies without apparent incident. And each year they add to the nest, landing with the utmost grace, twig in beak, only to be seen later kicking the same twig around in the most inelegant, inartistic fashion.

Behind these islands, to the north, lies the sweep of beach that marks Opitsaht. The Tla-o-qui-aht people who live here take their name from a village at the mouth of the Clayoquot River. *Tla-o-qui* means "different, changing"; *aht* means "people of." The Tla-o-qui-aht are part of the Nuu-chah-nulth ("all along the mountains"), a larger First Nations language group made up of 14 coastal tribes.

At the east end of the beach at Opitsaht is a channel, protected from southeasterly storms by the presence of Stockham Island. Its location gives Opitsaht many of the conditions necessary for a permanent village site: southern exposure, a broad sandy beach for launching canoes, a protected, deep-water harbour, a back way into Lemmens Inlet behind Stockham Island, Lone Cone mountain as a landmark and lookout, access to the Arakun mudflats for the hunting of geese and ducks, and access to the rest of Meares for fresh water for the fall run of chum and for hunting deer. Opitsaht had nearly everything that was needed by the Tla-o-qui-aht people. But, as with many of the important villages in the sound, little trace of the traditional structures exists.

What I see from here are two rows of modern houses, differentiated by colour. The Meares Island Cultural Centre – which holds the band office and the general gathering place – is significantly different from the other buildings. It is a larger, longhouse-style building. Once there may have been as many as 200 longhouses here – and many totem poles. But, as is the way with wood, these houses succumbed quickly when an American naval captain, Robert Gray, set fire to the village in 1792. Gray had been trading in Clayoquot Sound with his ship, the *Columbia Recidivi*, and decided to winter over to build another boat. At what is now called Adventure Cove, in Lemmens Inlet, he established what he called Fort Defiance and constructed the sloop *Adventure*. During his stay, relations with the Tla-o-qui-aht were not easy: he was living on their land and his intentions were not clear. Mutual suspicion bred more mutual suspicion. At one point there was a plot against him that was uncovered in advance and amounted to little. It was in retaliation that Gray ordered the village destroyed. John Boit, ship's officer for the *Columbia*, recorded the burning in his journal: "I'm very sorry to be under the necessity of remarking that this day I was sent with three boats all well manned & armed to destroy the village of Opitsahtah; it was a command I was in no way tenacious of & I'm grieved to think that Capt Gray should let his passions go so far."

Years later the village burned a second time, this time by accident, further eradicating any connection to its former appearance.

Following these early contacts, apparently commencing in the 1860s, Native populations up and down the coast were decimated by disease. In *The Adventures and Sufferings of John R Jewitt – Captive of Chief Maquinna*, Jewitt recalls his amazement at the lack of sickness he encountered when living with the Natives of the West Coast. Jewitt had been taken prisoner by the Mowachaht and lived with them for two years; during that time, there were very few deaths in the village. He also recalls how hardy the people were, and how able they were to survive intense cold – cold that he thought would surely kill him. These people were obviously healthy. They had never been exposed to widespread disease. Their oral history held no record of such disasters; they were completely unprepared for the devastating effects of epidemics. Diseases such as smallpox were virulent killers to begin with; their effect on Native people was terrible. Populations that had been stable for centuries were suddenly reduced in number to a mere few; entire families died; ancient burial practices had to be abandoned because no one was left to carry them out.

While Native people succumbed to the epidemics, Europeans began to settle more comfortably into the land, land that had never been officially ceded to them. Numerically weakened, physically and culturally shocked, and surrounded by ever-growing numbers of settlers, Nuu-chah-nulth voices of protest were muffled. The Nuu-chah-nulth have always had incredibly strong notions about ownership and personal rights. Land boundaries were always well defined and well respected. Yet it is only in the last few years that the provincial government has entered into treaty negotiations and gingerly acknowledged Native title to these lands.

As I peer across the water at the village of Opitsaht, I can just make out two totem poles, both carved within the last 10 years, symbolic of the recovery that is underway here. Not only is the population growing, but the Tla-o-qui-aht are taking part in many of the activities going on in Clayoquot Sound. I wonder how different things would be without Captain Gray and the epidemics. What would I be looking at now?

It's ironic that we're now heading to the scene of first contact – Clayoquot Island, site of the first trading post in the sound. This island is the one place that was agreed upon in dealings with the Tla-o-qui-aht. In the late 1800s it was traded for two barrels of molasses – a deal that would make today's realtors drool. Needless to say, the island is now worth many more barrels of molasses; it is a beautiful and diverse spot with sandy beaches, rocky shores and incomparable views of Meares Island.

We are heading toward the sandspit, where Adrian has seen a small group of birds, the same sandspit upon which the heads of 18 Kyuquot men were said to have been raised, on poles, by the Tla-o-qui-aht after a successful night raid. Thankfully, no whitened skulls loom over us today. Instead, our focus is on what's below us. The water is so shallow that we are paddling over a visible spread of underwater colour and life.

The point of travelling to a beautiful place is to enjoy the surroundings fully. Hardly what one could call a chore, but it's made even easier when the weather is fine. Here, the author and friend and fellow paddler Jan (right), stop to appreciate a moment of sunshine.

Everywhere there are white shells, large ones, from horse clams. And as with any location where clams abound, there are moon snails, their fantastic spiral shapes patrolling the sea floor, seeking out clam dinners. It is hard to imagine these snails as the tough predators they are, but like their cousins the slugs, they have hearty appetites and are willing to chew through most substances. Each snail is equipped with a radula, a long, oval-shaped tongue embedded with 27,000 teeth. As if using a drill, the snail bores into the clam with its radula, making a perfect hole, usually near the hinge of the shell. This is truly seafood dining "in the shell." Interestingly, it is a taste that they develop gradually. As young snails they are vegetarians, surviving on diatoms and sea lettuce. It is only later in life that they develop carnivorous tendencies.

Also abundant beneath us are the moon snails' egg collars. These weird objects have the most wonderful texture. About half a centimetre thick, and resembling a grey cloak, the shape of the snail's deceptively large, plump body, they are made as the snail exudes a slime that blends with the fine mud of its habitat. They provide the protection needed by the snail's young and are surprisingly resilient. As I pick one up I can only liken the material to the inner tube of a car tire – smooth and flexible, but strong. If I didn't know what this was, I would be here a long time trying to figure it out.

As we continue past the sandspit I float over an enormous, pink, five-rayed sea star, at least a foot across. But while Jan and I are looking at it, a small rock crab sidles over to the sea star and starts poking it from underneath. The fat pink arms move sharply (for a sea star) to protect its underside, where it is probably digesting a menu item – likely a mussel. The crab continues poking, using its biggest pincer in a gleeful onslaught. We feel like such voyeurs, examining the minutiae of these underwater lives, but the entertainment value makes it impossible to resist.

Finally we resume paddling, still close to the shore of Clayoquot Island, heading south. In the late 1800s, paddling to Clayoquot from Opitsaht might have meant that we were trading goods: sea otter furs or dogfish oil. Or a schooner might have come in and we could be offering to work on a pelagic sealing expedition, as did many of the young Native men.

But if it was after 1917, we might have been coming to meet the *Princess Maquinna*. This supply ship passed up and down the coast, usually coming through the sound on both the outgoing and return journeys, docking at both Clayoquot and

Tofino. At that time many of the settlers lived close to the water, or on islands, because it was much quicker and easier to get around by boat than it was to hike through the dense forest. When the *Princess Maquinna* sounded her horn, boats would appear from all over, converging in great excitement. Arriving were supplies that people had ordered the previous month. I try to imagine the anxiety of the moment: did I remember to ask for butter? Did I order enough flour, now that we have a visitor staying? Have I thought of everything I need for this month?

Then there would be the excitement of socializing, of seeing someone's newly arrived piano, or armchair, of catching up with friends, of seeing children, of receiving mail from far away.

Our mood in no way rivals the buzz of excitement that would have been going on when the *Princess Maquinna* arrived. Ours is an excitement of a different kind, a swelling sense of departure and adventure, a sense of relief at leaving mundane things behind. It has been a feat of planning to pack food for a week. Even thinking about planning groceries one month ahead, and sustaining ourselves in the interim, is a challenge.

There was much to life at Clayoquot; in fact, for many years the island was the hub of activity in the sound. There was a hotel, a school, stores, summer cabins – even a jail and a policeman. By comparison little existed at Tofino. But the island has always had a history of private ownership, so those who made their lives there did so by paying rent on any land they occupied. Eventually land became available for sale in Tofino and gradually the peninsula became the more popular place to live.

Clayoquot Island had a succession of owners who always maintained the hotel, which for many years held the only liquor licence in the sound. It wasn't until the 1980s that the hotel fell out of use. In 1990, just when it was about to slide down the sand dune upon which it was built and plunge into the sea, it was demolished. Today, there is a driftwood stage close to the site of the old hotel. Occasionally, open-air performances take place here, and there are few venues more lovely. The party-goers are invited to bring tents and stay over; in the space of an afternoon the beach mushrooms with multicoloured nylon shapes. Children run blissfully through the lawns and flowerbeds, while adults gather around an open fire, or dance to live music as the moon serenely rises over Mount Colnett, heavy and yellow with the heat and lushness of the summer.

At one point two sisters owned the island and operated the hotel. The island's reputation for its gardens – especially its rhododendrons – stems from their hard work. The present owner, Susan Bloom, has made these historical gardens her focus, restoring them, enhancing them and adding to them. Once a year she opens the gardens to the public, inviting everyone to bring a picnic, maintaining another link to the past: Clayoquot Days.

Historically, Clayoquot Days was an annual ritual that brought people together for competitions and games and sheer good fun. There were greased poles for adults to climb and foot races for the children; the different tribes competed in canoe races. It was an event of some magnitude, one that seemed to transcend human differences. If we'd been here then, the water would have been festooned with fishing boats, wooden rowboats and dugout canoes. Ladies and gentlemen would be walking up the pier with their families, dressed in their finest, bursting with the excitement of the occasion.

About 20 years ago the event was discontinued, and for a while it looked as if it would vanish into the annals of time. But in 1993 Susan Bloom revived it, including the canoe races and the children's games, and added live music events with well-known singers. Unfortunately, in this modern age of festival circuits, the party quickly became too popular, too huge and too far removed from its origins as a local celebration. The contemporary Garden Days, in May, retain the historical date of the occasion, but are a more manageable way to keep the flame alight.

What with the arrival of the *Princess Maquinna* and Clayoquot Days, this island has seen much festivity. But if places have seen happy times, they have, usually, also seen sadness. As we paddle past the long pier, which has somehow survived years of brutal onslaughts by storms, we see a forested area come into view, a place where a community of Japanese-Canadian fishermen once lived with their families. They built homes here in 1923 and survived by fishing commercially, using methods far more advanced than had been used in Clayoquot up to that time. It was the Japanese who pioneered the trolling technique that was so successful in salmon fishing. It caught on quickly. Trolling allowed a way of life that was accessible and appropriate for coastal people. Trollers didn't have to be huge boats – some of the Native people trolled from their canoes, filling them to the brim with salmon before rowing in to sell their catch, then rowing back out again. Trollers didn't have to go far afield; they could return to their families late every night and leave early every morning, instead of spending days at sea on bigger boats. The salmon fishery grew and grew, and by the 1960s and 1970s there was a real boom. But by the 1980s the stocks were declining and the prices had dropped dramatically. Every year it became harder to make a living.

In the past two years, the government has been buying back the trolling licences, which has pared down the fleet to a mere few and left fishing in the hands of huge seine boats that are corporately owned. The trolling technique is 100 years old this year and it seems to have come and gone. With the exception of a few working boats, the only trollers around these days are those that have been cheaply bought and converted for pleasure use. Just now, as I look to the south, there is a troller that I don't recognize heading out to sea. I feel like chasing after it and asking, *Where are you going? What are you doing?*

Long before the demise of trolling, however, at the time of the Second World War, the Japanese – regardless of whether they were first- or third-generation Canadians – were deemed Enemy Aliens and evacuated because of the wartime climate. In the early forties, this vibrant and hard-working community literally vanished, forced to leave the area they had become so much a part of, forced to give the government their homes, their boats, their belongings.

A reminiscence by Islay MacLeod in *The Sound* newspaper, recalls that time.

Time seemed to stop for me that day in Tofino. There were my friends, Emiko and her sister Sachiko . . . and there was the Japanese boy who had won a place in my heart forever by helping me with my Arithmetic. And there were all the others milling about on the Government wharf . . . I had never seen so many Japanese adults and children together at one time. It seemed to my young eyes that half the population of Tofino was leaving. And there we were, the other half . . . watching, watching, watching . . . as our former friends gathered their pitifully few belongings together. These friends who almost overnight became our enemy . . .

The C.P.R. ship, *Princess Maquinna*, arrived on that day looking drab and ominous in her wartime grey and soon my Japanese friends went up the gang plank, clutching their suitcases or possessions wrapped in snowy white cloths. Not one of them looked back and not one of them waved good-bye. The ship sailed and somehow the innocence of my youth and part of my heart went with it.

Not surprisingly, the Japanese-Canadians never returned. The government released them from their exile after the war ended. But the paranoia still existed, and was made manifest in 1947, when the Tofino council passed a motion disallowing Japanese-Canadians from owning land in the district. While European immigrants expected to be able to take this land from the Native people, they did not consider other cultural groups worthy of the same rights.

Any friendships that existed in 1947 would have been framed by a social context that deemed the Japanese second-class citizens. Where some Japanese people may have found kinship was with the Native people. Some of the older Tla-o-qui-aht speak fondly of their times with the Japanese. And while the two cultures might not have mingled much, there seems to have been genuine mutual respect. A few Japanese fishermen gave their fishing boats to Native people in anticipation of the day that they would be otherwise forced to relinquish them – to the government.

The emptiness that seems to float around the edges of the trees on Clayoquot Island may be the result of my thoughts: I am imagining how this place would feel if it were bustling with human life and community. How many homes were wrecked by this one paranoid act? Of course, Clayoquot Island was not the only place in the sound where Japanese-Canadians lived; there were other communities on the Esowista Peninsula that also vanished. But on Clayoquot Island, their departure in 1942 signalled the end of the community in general. There were too few people here now, others had moved to Tofino. Even the school closed, because the children had gone. After this, the island continued mostly as a resort. The bar and restaurant were popular, first, with men from the Long Beach airbase; later, they catered mostly to locals and the odd tourist.

Something moves, over on the rocks. It is a small raccoon, looking for mussels while the tide is low. Spying us, the little fellow stands up and peers out from behind his bandit mask, bright-eyed, full of curiosity, wringing his tiny hands. I try not to stare, having had good experiences with animals when they think they have not been seen. Instead I peek out of the corner of my right eye, before moving on down the channel with the tide.

The water is so clear here, and the seaweed that has been revealed by the low tide is reflecting rich blues and reds. The sky is still overcast, still with a hint of blue

opening up in the west. A little breeze is ruffling the water. We are at the very tail end of the ebb tide right now, its effects barely discernible, and are starting to cross an open area where we should be able to feel the ocean swell. There is obviously not much of one today and we lilt along, the breeze blowing away the intensity of the past, filling us with freshness and the present: the feel of the water under our boats, against our paddles, the delight of movement. Adrian asks what we should be naming this adventure and I suggest "Desperately Seeking Summer," a moniker we all easily relate to. We are paddling in a companionable group, chatting about this and that, relaxing into the trip.

Right now we are aiming towards Wickaninnish Island, named after a well-known Tla-o-qui-aht chief (although other chiefs before and since have shared the name). Wickaninnish is now owned by a group of shareholders, most of whom have cabins tucked into the edges of the forest, peeking out at the sea. At the tip of Wickaninnish lies the Tla-o-qui-aht summer village island of Echachis, once spanned by longhouses and used as a lookout for whales. The name is thought to mean "coming up out of the ocean," either in reference to the actual rising of the island after the glaciers had retreated and the forces of isostatic rebound were most noticeable, or to the way the island would seem to float above the water some days, when seen from Opitsaht, in the way of mirages.

To the west lies Vargas Island, our destination for today. In contrast to many of the large, mountainous islands in the sound, Vargas is distinctly flat, renowned for its wonderful sandy beaches. The distant beach I can see from here is Yarksis ("big beach"), which was the spring and summer home of the Kelsomaht. Although it is beautifully situated, facing southeast, in a good hunting area, Yarksis never survived as a village for many reasons, some of which are easier to pinpoint than others – the epidemics, for one. It is also thought that in the late 1880s many Kelsomaht men were lost during a pelagic sealing expedition.

Their numbers reduced, the Kelsomaht amalgamated with the Ahousaht. In later years, after demands for centralization were made by the Department of Indian Affairs, other tribes also amalgamated with the Ahousaht, occupying the site of Marktosis on Flores Island.

There is a physical drawback to Yarksis that has recently become apparent: it has no protected anchorage. The beach was fine for pulling up canoes, but gas-engine

A panoply of underwater delights: one of the rewards of paddling in shallow water.
Kayakers have the luxury of being able to cruise where other boaters cannot go.
There is nothing like a cruise through shallow water to get away from motorboats.

boats need safe, deep-water harbours. Once commercial fishing became a way of life, people moved away from many villages along the coast.

We cross Father Charles Channel to Moser Point, the boundary between Tla-o-qui-aht and Kelsomaht territory. There was said to have been an argument here over a drifting whale. Each group wanted it. Two ropes were tied to it with the canoes paddling in opposite directions. Eventually, the whale was cut in half to keep the peace. There are no whales here today, alive or dead, and any dead whales that drift in these days are snatched up quickly for research. In this open section of water, we try to keep our crossing as short as possible. The mild current and the calm, gentle sea have made it nothing too challenging, but it's not always like this. Father Charles Channel can pose some tricky situations for boaters, especially when the ebb tide is running and the standing waves build; throw in some wind and you have a perfect recipe for trouble. My respect for Father Charles Channel was born out of many crossings, the most memorable of which was the time I thought I was surely going to be carried far out to sea, helpless until the tide changed. Of course, I was fairly new to kayaking then, blissful in my ignorance. And while I'm still blissfully unaware of my ignorance, I try to make a point of not repeating my mistakes. Good judgment is a strange trait, though. Just when you think you can apply it, something happens to demonstrate how much more of it you need. My preference now is to take my time. (And always to pack enough food for an extra few days, the necessity of sticking to a schedule being a great obstacle to good judgment.)

Now, the conditions are phenomenal and my judgement is that we should make the most of them. So we float out to Wilf Rocks and admire the uniquely pale blue of the water and the silky rollers that pile up and come towards us. The mid-afternoon clouds have become puffy and white and they're breaking up as we sit here. There's another band of cloud on the horizon, but behind that is just blue sky. Could it be that the sun is coming out? Our hopes are rising, but we try to quell them, knowing that we've been disappointed all month. When the sun breaks through, however, we can't suppress our excitement – laughing and hooting like teenagers. We are close to our destination, so we head for the beach – all of us longing for a nap in warm sand and sunshine.

Medallion Beach, on Vargas, lies on both sides of a tombolo of sand, somewhat protected from the ocean by the collection of rocky islands called Wilf Rocks. It is not too well protected, however, and the surf is often a problem here, dumping steeply, close to shore. (Dumping unwary kayakers, too!) The tombolo reaches out to one of the islands, which can be accessed by scrambling over rocks and seaweed at low tide. Most of the spit is under water during high tide, so we lug the boats over to the main section of the beach, to the right, away from the spit. It's a long way, but we are full of energy, because the sun is out! Thrilled, we stride back and forth through the soft, sinky sand, carrying gear and gear and more gear, and finally, the boats. Then we collapse against a log and murmur peacefully about unimportant things before drifting away on a well-earned tide of sleep.

Sometimes it is as if a trip does not truly begin until after the first nap. Sleep is the ultimate form of letting go – the moment for releasing the details that keep you mentally tied to another place and time. So, as I emerge from a short, deep sleep I wake to the adventure at hand; I am truly in the moment. And at this moment, what has woken me is the passage of the sun behind the trees, which has transformed my warm patch of sand into a cool patch of shade. Jan and Adrian have moved themselves into the sun, but it is a losing battle; the shadows are hurrying down the beach.

A clean break: surf rushes shoreward at Medallion Beach, Vargas Island. This beach is often a challenge for launching and landing, especially with a loaded kayak.

We watch for a while as a rivalry plays out between two eagles and an osprey. In a seemingly unprovoked display of boldness, the osprey dives at one of the eagles, perched at the top of a tree. A brief skirmish ensues, ending in an impasse. But soon after this, the osprey is fortunate enough to catch a fish and the eagle takes revenge, diving on the osprey while it helplessly trails its catch, harassing it victoriously. I've seen these scenes play out so often; they never really amount to much. From time to time the osprey will lose its fish, but I have never witnessed physical injury – only injured pride.

While there is still light in the sky we decide to stretch our legs and walk in the forest. At the eastern end of the beach a small trail passes through the forest to a calm, rocky bay. Here the noise of the ocean is muffled, the quietness enhanced only by the melodious trilling of the Swainson's thrush. If we thought things had been peaceful before, we are now reevaluating. The atmosphere of the moment sinks deeply into us, refreshing us, filling us up. There is a feeling of openness in the forest. Sunlight glows in the spaces between the Sitka spruce trees, highlighting the moss that is deep and thick, transforming it to cushions of velvet in front of our eyes.

Ridges of beach sand decorate Medallion Beach, Vargas Island, at low tide. Such patterns can be altered overnight like an ever-changing kaleidoscope of shapes.

The combination of late afternoon sun and the exertion of the walk makes us warm, and a quick test shows that the water of this calm bay is not outrageously cold. Within minutes Jan and I are happily immersed, swimming around the bay and out to the rocks. Adrian hops in briefly too, so that all of us are feeling clean and refreshed as we walk back to camp.

As we're cooking supper and setting up camp, the sun sinks away into the night, flooding the sky with colour. We nestle into the sand around the small fire, cupping bowls of pasta with fresh vegetables and red pepper pesto, all delicious and well earned. I silently bless the capacious holds of the kayaks, which allow us to escape the multitude of freeze-dried packages so inevitable on hiking trips. At this moment I am marvelling at how much more "normal" I feel – whatever that means. As soon as I get away from my small-town life, it never ceases to amaze me that I have been captured there for so long. What keeps me there? I start to feel as if I should live as a nomad, wandering from island to island and beach to beach. But of course this feeling changes with the weather; today the advent of sun has sent our spirits soaring. Were it pouring with rain my thoughts might be quite different. In the world of my imagination, nomads don't live in rainy places.

Around us the voices of the Swainson's thrush spiral up through the canopy into the night, a musical theme that will permeate the trip. Adrian has noticed four species of thrush inhabiting this beach: Swainson's, varied, hermit and, of course, the robin. Apparently it is unusual for all four to be so close together. I have yet to hear the hermit thrush, a rare bird, whose song is said to be the most beautiful of them all. Right now, however, it is difficult to imagine anything more lovely than that which surrounds us.

After a much-desired ration of chocolate, we drift into our tents and into our dreams, clean, tired and well fed. It has been a superb day – truly an auspicious beginning to the trip.

Chapter Two
EXPOSURE

From Medallion Beach, via Ahous Bay, to Blunden Island

I N THE MORNING A BAND OF CLOUD SHADES THE BEACH WITH grey, but before there is time to feel depressed, it clears off, leaving only blue sky. The prospect of a full day of sun sets our starved bodies scurrying into action, packing up, making breakfast, looking for all those things that were stuffed despondently at the bottom of the bags: sunscreen, sun hats, lightweight clothing.

Adrian is out stalking sand dollars, also known as medallions, for that perfect photograph. In this light, selecting any one composition must be a challenge; there is beauty everywhere.

The weather forecast is calling for westerly winds, building to moderate strengths of 15 to 20 knots this morning, then dying off to become light and variable later on. In some situations 20 knots can be problematic, but I don't anticipate any difficulties today. There are many stopping places along our route if the wind and the tide prove too strong for us; right now there is barely a ripple, so the first leg of the journey to

A sand dollar, or medallion, graces the coarse sand of its namesake beach.
Belonging to the same family as seastars and sea urchins, these creatures live
in the sand under the pounding force of the waves.

Ahous Bay, further west along the Vargas coast, seems assured. Calm seas, however, should not be thought indicative of the day. Here, they mean only one thing: it is calm at the moment of observation. The speed of change never ceases to amaze me. Some winds build in the time it takes to launch a boat. In general though, on a typical West Coast summer day, the prevailing northwesterly wind shows its feathers near midday and increases throughout the afternoon, often lasting until the late evening, sometimes continuing through the night.

I am relieved that the swell is so diminished. The route along the outer coast of Vargas Island can be tricky. There are lots of rocks here, some of which lie submerged and invisible until one unique wave breaks over them in a sudden, violent moment. Kayakers call these rocks "boomers," in tribute to the noise the waves make breaking over them. Not only can the force of the wave be enough to overturn your boat, the prelude to the wave – the moment when the surge pulls the water backwards, exposing the rock – can leave a boat momentarily stranded, high and dry, completely at the mercy of the ensuing breaker and the barnacles beneath. Brand-new kayaks

A smug sense of satisfaction can wash through the early riser who has been rewarded by a colourful sunrise. Here, dawn glows over Wickaninnish Island and touches the wet sand of Medallion Beach, Vargas Island.

have been dashed to smithereens in this way, their paddlers equally shredded. It's not a pretty thing to contemplate, but it happens. Meticulous chart reading and constant watching can help avoid trouble. By scanning the water constantly, it's possible to pick out telltale places where the water peaks or swirls. Even then there can still be surprises. Faced with such unpredictable conditions the best hope is for quick reactions and the right instincts.

Right now there is so little swell that the surf is even gentle, rushing at the beach in small peaks, so different from the characteristic thump. The tide is fairly low and the tombolo stretches away, out to the island in a decorative crescent, the coarse grey sand of the beach scalloped with white, in the pattern of retreating waves. The last-quarter moon is still high in the sky, its white shape the only interruption in the welcome arc of blue.

I am amazed to see that Wilf Rocks are not frenzied with fishing boats. It's early morning and a beautiful day. The salmon must not be in yet at the Glory Hole. It's too early in the year – a year that has already shown itself to be slow. Some years I have counted more than 60 sport-fishing boats in one tiny spot, all of them hoping for The Big One. At times the commercial trollers are there too, adding to the melee, the potential for entanglement, the potential for argument. Commercial fishers are not always sympathetic to sport fishers, and vice versa, and the rivalry is enhanced by dwindling salmon stocks. But at the end of the day, fish are unloaded, weighed and displayed, and the pubs swell with people and stories, irritations usually forgotten, as long as the catch was good.

Thirty years ago there would have been few sport fishers here. The commercial industry was blossoming and trollers abounded. Smaller boats might have caught fish for home use, for smoking, canning or freezing; in some cases, they fished commercially as well. Tla-o-qui-aht hereditary chief Robert Martin recalls fishing commercially from a dugout canoe: "We'd row out to Wilf Rocks, or behind Lennard Island. It was a 14-foot canoe. I made it myself. When the fish were biting good, it used to take me about three or four hours to fill it up." He'd row in, offload his catch and row back out again. Robert started fishing when he was nine years old. His parents fished for a living, but he remembers them canning fish for food at the end of the season.

He also remembers the 1930s to the 1950s, when the season ran "from January for as long as you could stay out there – October usually. We could get 2,000 pounds a day. There was no limit. Any day, any time. It was only a dollar a licence. For a whole year, you could do whatever you wanted."

The contrast is stark: today fish are scarce, many areas have been closed and licences are prohibitively expensive. Today, the prices for salmon are low, due in part to competition from salmon farms.

Today you can't even see fish jumping.

That is a relief, in a way, because although I have brought my fishing gear and am dying to catch a fish, some of the salmon at Wilf Rocks are huge, and I'm wary of catching too much of an adventure. It's unlikely, but possible. There is an epic fishing story, recorded in *Sea Kayaker* magazine, about catching more than was expected. Four city slickers were kayaking in Kyuquot Sound. One of them caught a massive halibut – five feet, nine inches long – which created endless chaos and nearly upset all of them. The line wove around and through the boats, snagging on rudders, and eventually the halibut thrashed violently at the surface. Someone had to kill the halibut; someone had to get close enough to hit it "between the eyes." But halibut don't have an eye on either side of their bodies, they have two bizarrely positioned eyes on their topside, close together. Flummoxed, and stricken with panic, the men vainly attempted to look on the underside of the fish: "Where's the other eye?" Eventually, they discovered their primal instincts and managed to kill the beast. They towed it to a nearby beach and collapsed, before wondering what to do with 120 pounds of fish and no freezer.

The story of Eric the Halibut was printed years ago, but since reading it I have always been careful to choose small lures when fishing from my kayak. And with no fish visibly jumping right now, I hope no one will suggest that I try fishing. Besides, we should make the most of the conditions today and go while the going is good . . .

Refreshed by the crispness of the day, our packing goes quickly. We haul the gear down the beach with vigour, and pack the boats more efficiently, now that we've established the best places for things. Each of the kayaks is a slightly different shape, with a different holding capacity. The gear is divided into group (food-related) gear and personal possessions. Most of the group gear is in regular nylon stuff sacks lined with garbage bags, but the personal gear is more cautiously stored in dry bags – keeping clothes and sleeping bags dry is vital. The beach is momentarily splashed with

Southeastern Vargas Island bares its jagged teeth. During storms these rocks virtually disappear behind explosions of white spray as the ocean meets the land. In this photo, the sandy curve of Medallion Beach can be seen in the background, taking refuge behind Wilf Rocks.

colour as we examine the chaos and stash it away, bag by bag. Despite years of paddling experience, I am constantly amazed by the mountain of equipment that can disappear into a kayak. A boat can be a regular magician's hat of surprises. I have yet to see anyone produce a white rabbit out of their hatch, but there have been occasions that certainly came close.

Once, leaving the beach in Kyuquot, a guest began to scream uncontrollably in her boat. Arms flailing wildly, she seemed sure to capsize. But what was the matter with her? She was obviously incapable of telling us. As we got her to the beach she catapulted herself out of the boat and started to run around frantically, randomly. And as we looked at her boat, an equally confused, equally frantic, very small grey mouse skittered out of the cockpit and galloped willy-nilly up the beach, to the safety of the logs.

It is always a good idea to check for overnight kayak visitors – especially since you could find yourself sharing your seating arrangements with them. Satisfied that I have my boat to myself, I pull on my well-worn spray skirt and life jacket and look around for something cotton with which to wipe my sunglasses. Even though it's such a comfortable, tempting fabric, I try not to take cotton on paddling trips. It's renowned for its cooling properties; once wet, it can strip the warmth from your body in minutes. It can be a huge contributing factor in hypothermia; on a less dramatic scale, it can be just plainly unpleasant. Kayaking clothes always get wet. It's the rule rather than the exception. When you get into a boat, water drips off your shoes into the cockpit; a boat wake can send a splash down the front of your body; small choppy seas can saturate your spray skirt – and eventually you. Paddling in damp, cold clothes seems perverse, especially when there are new, quick-drying fabrics available that are warmer and more comfortable. The only problem with the new fabrics is that they are useless for cleaning sunglasses – but I'll take that problem over hypothermia any day.

We launch the boats safely and paddle towards the rocky headland lying southwest of us. Squeezing through a tiny passageway in the rocks, we enter a large tidal pool. The kelp and surf grass wave gracefully beneath us, but we are focusing on the rocks, looking for harlequin ducks. These rare birds are often found here, decorating the scenery with their costumelike black and white plumage. Their habits are mysterious, and finding them is a matter of luck. Today they are elsewhere.

Continuing through the passageway to more open water, we come into an area that the whale-watching fraternity calls Orca Alley, a combination of water, kelp beds and rocks that provides an attractive habitat for seals. The orcas that frequent the West Coast are transients – genetically separate from the large, gregarious pods of resident orcas found on the east coast of Vancouver Island. While resident orcas eat mostly fish, transients prey on marine mammals such as seals, sea lions, porpoises – sometimes even grey whales. Transients usually travel in small groups, tracking down prey in a combination of under- and above-water searches. I have seen them "spy-hop" – come slowly up out of the water to survey their surroundings, and check for unwary seals basking on the rocks. I have been closely examined in this way myself, although I was in a motorboat at the time. I am thankful to have escaped excessive scrutiny from the orcas on those occasions when I have seen them from a kayak.

Needless to say, the sight of an orca on the hunt can be dramatic; many unfortunate seals and porpoises have been seen – quite literally – being shaken out of their skins ("tenderized," as an old-timer jokingly told me once). Even though no incidents of orca aggression towards kayakers have been recorded, orcas still inspire a healthy dose of fear. Observing them can be the pinnacle of experience with wildlife, especially from such a small boat.

I have become lazy about looking for whales in recent years. A sure sign of their presence is the accompanying swarm of whale-watching boats. And since there are no boats around us at the moment, I find myself more concerned about possible boomers than seeking out orcas. At best, the transient orcas are sporadic in their visits to Clayoquot Sound, and while some whale watchers have been lucky enough to see grey whales, orcas and humpbacks all in one day, life is not often so exciting. My blood is not coursing with adrenaline right now, but I am awash with a strong sense of appreciation for the weather and the surroundings, filled with the pleasure of adventure. I can see the tops of Lone Cone, Mount Colnett and Catface peeking out over the treeline of Vargas. As landmarks they are conspicuous, orienting us to our position in relation to the rest of Clayoquot Sound. We paddle toward a large, domed rock and venture in amongst the smaller rocks and kelp at its base. The kelp is at a young stage in its growing cycle, a moment when its green-gold colours seem strong. The way the light falls across the blades enhances their graceful sweep and draws in the eye. A little further on, the rocks beneath us are polka-dotted with green sea anemones and red sea urchins.

Clinging to life: although it looks serene, claiming a place in the intertidal zone can be a fight to the finish. Much tenacity is needed, not only to withstand the movement of the water, but also to squeeze into any available niche.

The dark red spines of the sea urchins form an impressive armour against which their predators – humans and sea otters – have to contend. Human predators come in the form of commercial divers, who bring the sea urchins to the surface, where they are quickly shipped to Japan for large sums of money. Sea otter predators are motivated purely by their physical appetites, which are substantial. Last year, a sea otter was sighted in Clayoquot Sound on several occasions – the first to be seen in many years. Once they were a conspicuous feature of the outer coast scenery. But between the 1740s and the early 1800s, three quarters of the sea otter population was wiped out, in a gold-rush-style onslaught of hunting. Initially it was the Russians who traded with the Natives for sea otter pelts, but in a short time, an international free-for-all developed, with outrageously high prices being fetched for the pelts in China, Saint Petersburg and London. By 1911 the tattered remnants of a once-vibrant population were granted international protection, but this did not stop all the poaching. The last sea otters on the Canadian coast were poached to extinction in the Queen Charlotte Islands in the 1920s.

With no sea otters to prey on them, sea urchins have proliferated, spreading along the seashore, grazing on kelp and other seaweed. And because they graze from below, they can eradicate large areas of kelp, changing their surroundings quite dramatically. Such colonies are like underwater deserts. They are known as "urchin barrens."

At four to four and a half feet, sea otters are the smallest of the true marine mammals, but they are set apart from them by their lack of a thick, insulating layer of fat. Instead, sea otters keep themselves warm by means of their voracious appetites and luxurious fur coats. To create heat through caloric intake, they consume about a third of their body weight daily. But to insulate themselves, they must maintain a layer of air within the fibres of their fur. The reason for the popularity of sea otter fur is that, at 700,000 hairs per square inch, it is the densest fur of any mammal. The density allows for maximum retention of air, but condemns the sea otter to a life of grooming. Its hairs must be kept perfectly clean to maintain their insulating quality and buoyancy.

In 1969, 29 sea otters were reintroduced to the West Coast from Amchitka Island, Alaska. They were released in Checleset Bay, close to the Brooks Peninsula, north of Clayoquot. The area was then protected to allow the reintroduction to be successful. Transporting the otters was risky; many died, their fur having become soiled during the process of travelling. Several other reintroduction attempts followed, until gradually the population took hold. The otters have since flourished, easily becoming acclimatized to their once-natural habitat. The transplants have gradually spread along the coast. There is a healthy population to the northwest, at Estevan Point, a day away by motorboat. Barring unforeseeable disasters such as oil spills, sea otters should soon reinhabit Clayoquot Sound. When that happens, the tableau beneath me might look different: where there are urchins, there might be kelp, and where there is kelp, there might be sea otters – lying on their backs, holding rocks on their tummies, diligently cracking open their lunches, warming their flippers, playing with their young, charming their onlookers.

Adrian found a dead sea otter on Medallion Beach last year. Marvelling at the quantity of sea urchins here currently, he wonders out loud if the sea otter he found might not have died from gluttony. It's anyone's guess. But there are many who consider sea otters to be pests because of their appetite for shellfish such as abalone. Sea otter deaths can unfortunately have more sinister causes than gluttony – misplaced resentment and ignorance can make them targets for humans with guns.

At this moment we are close to the place where I saw last year's lone sea otter. It isn't here now of course, but we have been lucky enough to spot three harlequin ducks. We are coming up to Ahous Point and at midday it's still flat calm! There's a bit of a wind ripple, but overall we are being extremely spoiled. At Ahous Point, the lime-green meadow grass is at its most verdant. The spruce stand out from the other trees, with their new, pale green tips, and I can see the coarse, sandy tips of dune grass poking up around the logs, the sharp edges waiting to slice the legs of unwary walkers in shorts. Overhead, an osprey glides, checking the shallow water for fish.

We slip through the protective rocks that shield us from the Pacific swells. As we round the point, now heading northeast but still following the Vargas coast, two of the prettiest little bays in Clayoquot Sound lie on our right. They are part of the Ahous Point Indian Reserve, twin entrances to a single beach. Tucked away, facing west and north respectively, these bays are calm, reflecting the name Ahous, which means "facing away from the ocean." Little surf pounds the beach; truly, it is a perfect place to live. As with Opitsaht and Kelsomaht, there is barely a trace of the village that existed here. Only the trees give the secret away. A line of them, conspicuously smaller than the surrounding forest, has grown where longhouses once stood. But this place was an essential part of Ahousaht territory. When the weather was nice enough, families would have gathered all their possessions together and paddled out here from their permanent village sites. Boards that planked the sides of the winter longhouses would have been taken down and laid across the canoes, linking several of them together in a big raft. The same boards would then be placed on the existing frameworks of the summer houses and – hey presto! – there would be a village.

Several hundred years ago, the Ahousaht territory included most of the west side of Vargas Island, Calmus Passage and the Cypress Bay area. These are all beautiful areas, but only one of them, Cypress, had a salmon-producing river. For a tribe whose population was growing, having access to only one river was a severe limitation. In the early 1800s, the Ahousaht decided to provoke a war with one of their neighbours in order to increase their territory and gain access to more salmon-bearing rivers.

At first they attempted to provoke the Tla-o-qui-aht, but when there was no response, they reconsidered. The Tla-o-qui-aht had only three salmon-bearing rivers, whereas the O-tsus-aht, to the north, had many more. The O-tsus-aht lived across the water, along the southern and eastern parts of Flores Island and in Millar Channel and Herbert Inlet. Their name stems from their main summer village, O-tsus ("water gets into the bay"), which was situated at Siwash Cove, on the west side of Flores Island.

Eventually, the Ahousaht were successful in their provocations, and war broke out between them and the O-tsus-aht. It was a long war, and a bloody one, but it brought the Ahousaht what they sought: increased territory and greater access to salmon. Marktosis, the current site of the village of Ahousaht, was once O-tsus-aht land. Only the name was retained; there are few other present-day links to the historic existence of the O-tsus-aht.

Despite the war and the newly acquired lands, Ahous Point did not lose its importance. In the late spring the Ahousaht moved to the outer coast to fish for halibut and cod. This was also a time of harvesting intertidal creatures such as sea urchins, black turban snails and chitons, as well as large quantities of mussels. Springtime marked the beginning of the hunting season for marine mammals such as seals, sea lions, porpoises and whales. While the hunters of the smaller mammals brought in a substantial portion of the food needed, the small-mammal hunt had less importance than the whale hunt. Enormous spiritual significance was attached to the whale hunt and much ritual purification took place before one of them, large

Venturing forward: the kayaks seem dwarfed by the scenery along the southern coast of Vargas Island.
Ahead of these boats the Pacific stretches away, uninterrupted, towards the Asian continent.

portions of which were secret and very elaborate. The responsibility for hunting whales was considered to be the most noble of callings.

Ahous Point is perfectly located as a lookout spot for whales. The spring migration of grey whales passes just beyond the protective wall of the reefs through which we have just travelled. Whale spouts – those tall plumes of water vapour – are easily visible from the point. It is said that the canoes would wait among the reefs for a whale to go by before paddling out to it. Whale hunting was no small endeavour. The whaling canoes were about 32 feet long and were equipped with a long yew-wood lance, a harpoon head made of mussel shells and antler, and a number of seal-skin floats. The harpooner was a man of enormous importance – the hunt's success lay in his ability to inflict as much damage to the whale as possible at the outset. There was usually a crew of eight, each man with a specific job. There is evidence that the harpooners were very accurate when the canoe was brought into the range of a whale. Among the whalebones that have been discovered at midden sites are shattered shoulder blades (scapulae). The harpooner's blow was only the beginning of the battle, however. Whaling canoes were often towed great distances by the whale, completely at the mercy of the animal's superior strength. The hunters must have hoped that the whale would tire before they lost sight of land. Peter Webster, an Ahousaht elder, tells of one canoe being towed a distance of about 20 miles, from Bartlett Island (two miles west of Vargas) to Wickaninnish Bay, where the whale was speared a second time. But instead of slowing down, the whale headed far out to sea. By the time it died, the crew could see only the tops of Vancouver Island's snow-capped peaks for reference. Not only that, they ran out of food and water while they were attempting to tow the whale back to the coast. They were saved when they encountered a sealing crew who shared provisions with them. As they came closer to home, other canoes helped with the tow. The whole excursion took two weeks.

When the whale was brought back, it was carefully divided among the people, each family having claim to specific portions of it. Little was left unused. Interestingly, although the hunters were greatly respected, great respect was also bestowed upon the whale. Rather than extolling their own prowess, the hunters thanked the whale for giving itself to them and acknowledged the superior power they attributed to the whale.

Grey whale hunting took place during the spring migration, but resident grey whales also linger along the coast of Vancouver Island during the summer, finding enough food to sustain them during their later migration to the south. When first in Clayoquot Sound, I worked as a guide on a whale-watching boat. Three times a day we travelled to Ahous Bay to see the resident whales. Sometimes there would be up to a dozen of them there, each with their own spot, each one diving down to the sandy bottom and sucking in great mouthfuls of mud before straining the amphipods and crustaceans from it, each one apparently ambivalent about the others around it – breathing, diving, feeding, breathing, diving, feeding.

That was 1990; that summer, and the next, the whales fed constantly at Ahous Bay. Then abruptly, as if tired of it, they stopped. In recent years they have been alternating between Grice Bay, in Tofino Inlet, and areas along the west side of Flores Island. Perhaps the sea floor here at Ahous is being left to fallow until such time as it becomes productive again. I hope so. It would be a shame if the whales never graced this lovely bay again.

Despite the lack of whale-watching boats I find myself scanning for spouts – those elusive towers of mist that hang in the air just milliseconds longer than the spray from a breaking wave, that inspire so much excitement and awe among humans. Somehow it still seems improbable that there are no whales here; surely there is one hiding in a corner somewhere. But, no. Not this year. Next year, I find myself hoping, next year. Meanwhile, the mesmerizingly blue water is beautiful enough, whales or no whales. In fact, the water is so lovely it seems a shame to leave it so soon, but it is time to occupy ourselves with our own next mouthfuls. The subliminal call for lunch is about to become audible. Perhaps it is because the beach is in sight and it is obviously time to land.

We are now coming to Ahous Beach. It was tempting to land at one of the two smaller bays, but we didn't. They're part of the reserve. The government has allotted such tiny reserves to the Natives, who once had such an expansive territory; trespassing there would have been selfish and insensitive.

I prefer to see beyond the letters I. R. (Indian Reservation) on the charts, to the big picture, to consider this entire area traditional land. I hope the current treaty negotiations will come to the same conclusion, but since parts of Vargas Island have been recently declared a provincial park, it might not happen. Perhaps an agreement similar to the one regarding parts of the Queen Charlotte Islands will be reached; there, the province and the Natives share in managing of the park. Meanwhile, in the context of existing lines and boundaries, we land outside the reserve, on the main section of beach that fringes Ahous Bay at the southern end, where the surf is smallest. This beach is a sweeping semicircle of sand – a broad salute to life. Unfolding my cramped knees from the cockpit, I wish the stiffness away. I want to whirl around, arms outstretched, mimicking the wideness of the beach. I want to savour the sense of freedom as it slips through my fingers, as always, there and gone, there and gone.

The tide will be coming in for a while, so we have to carry the boats up the beach. This is the disadvantage of wide, sandy beaches; they tend to have such shallow inclines that the boats need to be hauled along for what seems like miles to set them out of reach of the tide. And at lunchtime, it is not practical to unload all the gear, which leaves the option of heaving them at full weight. Non-kayakers are often mistaken about the reason kayakers develop bad backs. It's not from all the paddling; it's nearly always from carrying boats! I wander over to the logs, my back still curved over. It eventually returns to an upright position when it trusts that no further weight lifting is in store.

Everything to do with lunch is in a red bag, the reason being that red is the most conspicuous colour, the one most people are likely to remember, so searches for lunch materials are not endless and time consuming. Today we find that nothing has been misplaced; before long we are busily munching on a selection of delights that are just one variation on an eight-day theme of crackers and tortillas, dips and relishes, cheeses and seafood, vegetables and fruit. Repetition notwithstanding, lunches are one of my favourite paddling meals, little bits of this and that, all combined with the reward of a break that promises exploration and relaxation and, today, sunshine.

As we slouch like rag dolls in the sun, a small plane lands on the sand a little way off. Two people emerge and walk purposefully down the beach. It is somewhat irritating that these people have been transported here with so little physical effort, just dropped out of the sky into the little piece of wilderness that we had considered temporarily our own. They have the air of afternoon walkers who must get the trip done before dinner. They stride past us, heading straight for the trail to the reserve, nodding a curt hello. They have obviously been here before. I try to imagine what it would be like if I had always lived here and never seen a plane. Would I have hidden from these people, fearful that they were aliens? Hmmm, the daydream progresses – maybe they are aliens. That little two-wheeler plane could actually be a very sophisticated space-travel module . . .

After lunch, we walk down the beach, heading for the lagoon. It feels so good to stretch our legs and move without restriction. We stride along, into the freshening breeze, hopeful in our anticipation of a swim.

A short while into the walk, we pass a colourful collection of crab-trap markers hanging off a pole. These indicate the entrance to the telegraph trail that crosses Vargas to the east side, near Kelsomaht. The trail was part of a telegraph system that ran the length of the west coast of Vancouver Island, constructed in 1903 for the purpose of saving lives. Not only were there many shipwrecks along the west coast, but in midwinter, any survivors who were lucky enough to make it as far as the shore were seldom able to go any further in the dense forest. The telegraph wire was supposed to be a way of calling for help. Further down the coast, south of Bamfield, there were also shipwreck cabins and call boxes that tapped into the wire. On Vargas there was no shipwreck cabin, but the wire followed a pioneer wagon trail that crossed the island from Ahous Bay, on the southwest side, to Mill Bay, on the east side, where homesteads existed and help was more accessible. The importance of the telegraph faded over the years as radio communications improved, but the trail is still used by locals and tourists alike. Recently, the new Vargas Island provincial park officials closed the trail, claiming that it was dangerous. Bridges were pulled out. Signs were erected, informing people of the closure. But the trail has not been repaired or brought up to standard since then.

The trail poses a dilemma for the park, however; although the trail passes through park land on the west side of Vargas, the only way to access it on the east side is through Kelsomaht Reserve or the private lands of the Vargas Island Inn. The inn is owned by Neil and Marilyn Buckle and is a true West Coast refuge, completely unaffected by the glitzy tone that is becoming pervasive in Tofino. The Buckles used to own Comber's Resort on Long Beach (at a spot now referred to as Comber's Beach). After Pacific Rim National Park expropriated their land, they moved to Vargas to operate a small woodlot and sawmill. Eventually, they opened their home to guests again. And once again, a park has moved in alongside them. This time, they have not been asked to leave. But part of the allure of the Vargas Island Inn has been the trail to Ahous – the trail that is now closed. Currently the situation has reached a stalemate, and some people find their way across the island anyway, trail or no trail. Obviously, the trail would be safer if it were maintained, which would be in keeping with its original intent.

The trail crosses an extensive area of bog that makes up a large part of the centre of Vargas. This environment is home to some unique and delicate plant species, such as the round-leaved sundew, a small insect-eating perennial similar to the Venus flytrap. The bog is also an indicator of the interesting geological history of the island. Vargas is thought to have been (prior to glaciation), two smaller, closely situated rocky islands. After the glaciers retreated, forces of isostatic rebound caused the land to rise up and spring back when released from the weight of the ice. Some of the land that rose up was once a beach. This sandy land became trapped between the two rocky areas and, since it lay at a lower elevation than the surrounding land, drainage was a problem, hence the bog.

We walk toward the lagoon, where some drainage does exist. Here, two creeks issue out to the sea. It is an interesting spot because the sea floods the lagoon at a high tide, changing it from a huge, sandy expanse, with small streams converging and trickling through it, to a vibrant, moving body of water. This is one of the few places

Sitka spruce often grow with remarkable uniformity and symmetry in sheltered watersheds, while in coastal locations they may rebel and become fantastic shapes. It is common for them to develop immense horizontal limbs, as with this tree on Vargas Island.

*Common Red Paintbrush (*Castilleja miniata*): a treasure trove of colour brightens the late-spring coastline. The fact that a sparse environment can produce such verdant growth makes the discovery of spring flowers even more special.*

46

on Vargas where fresh water exists; for that reason, I expect to find wildlife here, especially around dawn and dusk.

We cut onto a small trail where a rocky headland transects the beach, then cross another small section of beach, then go through some dune grass and reach the lagoon. Well, it would be generous to describe this as a "lagoon" at the moment. It is not high tide and not a good time for a swim. We sit at the top of a steep bank of sand, surveying the paltry brown creek beneath us. Grey sand stretches away from us in a desolate, otherworldly scene. In places, the sun-bleached limbs of dead trees decorate the emptiness with additional starkness. The sun beats down on our backs and the wind showers us with fine sand. If we sit here any longer we are going to turn into sand dunes, so we slide down the soft bank and wade across the creek to explore the wasteland.

On the other side of the creek my feet squelch over dark, sandy mud, which rises up everywhere in minivolcano-like shapes, complete with craters, suggesting subterranean dwellers of some sort. The higher areas are carpeted with thick pads of sea asparagus, their new shoots looking plump, ready for picking. Later in the year the shoots become too woody and do not make for good eating. Sea asparagus is sold as a specialty food; it graces gourmet plates and adds a few dollars to their price. Here it grows like a weed.

Further up the more western creek, a furlike algae coats the mud in vivid, fluorescent green. It feels like wet velvet beneath my toes. Looking back, I find the scenery picturesque: two creeks converge under a dark blue sky, there is a foreground of bright green, the wind ruffles the grasses on the banks of the other creek in a gentle, constant motion. Jan and Adrian are busy composing photographs. We can't stay long, however; the tide is coming in. As we regain the place of our crossing, we have to hold our shirts up high; we can see the increase in the current. Any longer and we would have been in for a challenging time.

Back on the beach, the wind has definitely increased. The surf is foamier and little whitecaps splatter the bay. Walking nearer the high-tide line we come across the skeleton of a deer, lying at the edge of the dune grass. Evidence of deer on Vargas is plentiful; there seem to be enough deer to support an almost permanent pack of wolves. More often than not I see deer tracks here. On several occasions the deer tracks have been closely followed by wolf tracks. I don't doubt that wolves pulled down this deer. There are signs that it was young and healthy, not old and diseased: a shiny hoof, some lustrous hair on the lower leg. The remains are oddly beautiful lying here in the sand and the grass, a reminder of the natural order of things.

Meandering back to the boats, we discuss the next leg of the route. The plan had been to paddle to the northwestern part of Open Bay to a sheltered, smaller bay within it. From there, we could hike further into the evening, over to another beach to watch the sunset. But while we were having lunch, we saw a motorboat drop off a large group of kayakers at the very bay to which we were planning to paddle. The beach is small, and not suited to quantities of people. It wouldn't be appropriate to camp there now, which leaves us two options. Either we can stay where we are and add an hour onto our journey to Flores tomorrow, or we can head over to Blunden Island, an hour's paddle west across the bay. Once there, we could hike across the island to the western shoreline, which is almost entirely shielded from the ocean by clusters of rocks. Being fresh to the trip and having paddled only three miles today, we decide to continue to Blunden in the late-afternoon breeze.

We untie the boats from their hitching logs and prepare for wetness on the crossing. I pull on my faithful paddling jacket and cinch up the strap to my hat. The wind is not all that strong – between 10 and 15 knots – but conditions seem worse than they are in reality because the wind is blowing against the tide, creating choppy surface water. It's important to assess how hard the wind is actually blowing, because wind is usually the kayaker's worst foe.

We launch easily in the small surf, paddling into the sparkling blue and white water. The waves are short and steep, and slap our bows down and wet our spray skirts. Conditions like these fill me with energy, as if the breeze has seeped under my skin and pumped new doses of life into me. I love all the splashing and movement. It's fun to guess where each wave will break and try to avoid a soaking. And as long as the wind isn't blowing us backwards, we're all right. As we anticipated, the wind isn't too bad; it pushes mildly against our paddle blades. It increases a little as we cross, just enough to make us look forward to the finish line.

On the east side of Blunden Island protective arms of land embrace a circular bay, very protected, calm and quiet. We slide through the lowering rays of sun to our landing places and quickly unload the boats. We have to carry them a shorter distance this evening, which is an added bonus. Since it is getting late in the day, we start cooking some rice and then bury the pot in the sand to keep it hot while we bushwhack over to the west side. The trail is heavily overgrown and difficult to find; clearly it hasn't seen much use in the last year or two.

We can see the sun from the outer shore once we get there and, once again, there is just enough heat left in the day to encourage us to plunge into the tranquil waters about the rocks. Adrian demurs this time, mentioning something about "hardy souls," but denied a swim at lunchtime, Jan and I are happy to have the cool bath that peps us up for supper.

We return in the last of the light as a hermit thrush sings in the distance. Jan and Adrian listen intently. I am further into the bush and can hear it only faintly, not so well that I would recognize it if I heard it again.

Near the beach on which we have landed are other small beaches, covered with mussel shells, that point to a history of Native use. Blunden would have acted as a satellite camp to the village at Ahous Point. There is little evidence of longhouses here, but no lack of signs of activity. Unlike the Ahousaht, we haven't harvested any mussels today nor, for that matter, any chitons. While mussels can be delicious, I have found chiton an acquired taste – an acquired activity, actually, since so much chewing is involved. Tonight our chewing activity involves a vegetable curry. It promises to be absolutely delicious, but coming as it does, after last night's vegetable pasta, the choice prompts cries for protein. I valiantly promise to catch a fish tomorrow to relieve the cravings of these well-exercised bodies.

Once more, night falls at suppertime. Our 9:30 p.m. dining hour is late, but it feels good to have made such full use of the day. We need to reserve some energy for tomorrow however, since there are two stretches of open water to cross, both of which may be problematic. But we'll find out what we're up against after assessing the weather in the morning.

From our camp, we look east towards Ahous. Calm pools of water in front of the beach reflect deep colours; the waters of Open Bay are still ruffled. The flat land of Vargas glows with soft light and the still-snowy peaks of the coast mountains begin to be tinged with pink. We are at the end of a long and satisfying day. It is a pleasure to set up the tent and settle in for the night. Blunden's atmosphere is soothing, serene amidst the lively waters.

Chapter Three
CROSSINGS

From Blunden Island, via Whaler Islet,
to Whitesand Cove, Flores Island

THE LAST SIX MONTHS HAVE MADE IT ALMOST IMPOSSIBLE TO be optimistic about the weather. The old adage is that if it seems too good to be true, it probably is. Our day and a half of sun has made me suspicious, so suspicious that I wake up early, uneasy about the conditions. I almost don't want to look out of the tent, but the humbug in me can't resist. When I look, the wind is coming from the north, which is unusual; winds from this directions are sometimes associated with outflow winds in the winter. It's not a heavy wind, but it provides food for thought as I watch it ruffle the open water beyond the bay.

When I turn on the VHF radio, I find that the weather forecasters are obviously confused, too. The marine forecast calls for light northerlies, followed by light variable winds, followed by moderate northwesterlies, followed by 20-knot southerlies. My guess is that they are expecting some sort of front, but don't really know when, or what effect it will have. I look to the clouds for more decision-making arsenal.

The common ochre seastar is a daunting intertidal predator. Seastars have an appetite
for seafood "in the shell." After using suction to establish an opening, they extrude
their stomachs right into the shell of the hapless victim where they then digest their meal.

They are a mixture: small and puffy, dragging little tails behind them, visibly moving. The sun, when it hits us, is intense. I wonder if we are in for some thunder.

Regardless of the changeable nature of the day, the wind is not expected to rise above speeds that will inhibit our paddling; in fact, a southerly wind, if it happens, will push us in the right direction. My extra dose of concern for the day is based on the two open-water crossings that await us. Paddling away from the shore always increases the danger quotient. You leave behind the possibility of being able to land quickly in an emergency. Crossings involve large expanses of open water; the larger the expanse, the more space over which the wind can build and the longer the exposure to strong, sometimes exhausting currents.

There will be, in fact, three crossings today; one of them is this morning's passage from Blunden to Vargas, but it should be quicker and less involved than the other two. The first big crossing for the day is Brabant Channel, between Vargas Island and Whaler Islet. This one should go well because we look set to have calm conditions for a little while. The crossing itself should only take just over an hour. I am more

Slipping through the clouds on silky morning water. There are moments when the movement, colour and texture of water can make paddling a sheer physical delight.

preoccupied with Russell Channel, the second section of open water, from Whaler Islet to Flores Island. With a northwesterly rising, we could find ourselves paddling directly into the wind. Fortunately the tide will be going our way by then, flooding in and providing smoother surface-water conditions than the ebb tide, which flows against the northwesterly.

These bubbles of thought rise and brew continually during the morning's activities. The three of us are busily occupied in one way or another: making breakfast, putting away tents, considering what to wear for the day and what gear to have close at hand. The tranquil bay absorbs the flurry of human motion and remains unaffected. Its protective curve is punctuated only by a gnarled hemlock that hangs out over the water on the far right-hand side of the beach. Further back from the water, but in the same area, there is a towering spruce covered with unusual, pinkish lichen. A few hundred yards from the beach a small island is already lit with sun, its tiny shell beach glowing whitely, trees behind it.

In the forest to the north of our camp, trails lead to the small shell beaches that are close by. The sheer quantity of mussel shells on these beaches is impressive; as I walk along them a satisfying crunch accompanies my every footstep.

We have been doing well. It's still early when we haul the boats and the gear down the beach. Sometimes the packing can go smoothly; other times it seems to take forever. Today we got up at seven o'clock and were prepared to move quickly. I'm glad, because we're now setting off in delightful conditions. Whatever transpires with the weather later in the day, the morning is stunning. After packing the boats and doing a final check to make sure nothing has been left behind, we have only to stretch the muscles with which we have lately become so well acquainted. A few groans later, we are off into the sharpening colour of the morning. We paddle through the handful of little islands that guard the exit like sentinels. The water has become glassy, the reflections intense. A roar of surf echoes out across the water from a windswept beach on Vargas. As we paddle towards the sound, a surging swell rolls underneath us, pushing us shoreward. I feel that familiar sense of connectedness – the melting of boundaries between body, spirit and water. I drink in the intensity of the colour, the sensation, the movement, the unique feeling of being a harmonious part of something beyond the self. It makes me want to go forever, just to continue feeling the water under my boat and swirling against my paddle blade. At the same time,

I don't want to go beyond the moment. I want to stay here, with this lovely, lilting swell whooshing up underneath me, pushing me over towards Vargas.

To minimize the time spent crossing open water, we go to Vargas first, before heading off to Whaler Islet. By doing so we eradicate any chance of seeing the Steller's sea lions at Plover Reefs, southwest of Blunden. This suits me perfectly. The sea lion is one marine mammal I prefer not to see when I am kayaking. They are huge, unpredictable beasts that carry their territory with them wherever they happen to go. Several incidents between sea lions and kayakers have occurred in Clayoquot Sound. They have not been fatal, but they have usually involved the sea lions unexpectedly ramming boats, like one-tonne submarine torpedoes. On one occasion a sea lion grabbed and destroyed a paddle.

Sea lions are gregarious creatures. It is usually a sea lion that is the sleek black animal at a circus, balancing a ball on its nose, crying, "Aark! aark! aark!" They are fantastically graceful in the water, swirling and gliding, as elastic as eels. Out of the water they are less appealing. Steller's sea lions are the largest. Elephant seals and walruses are the only other marine mammals that are larger, excluding whales. In Clayoquot Sound, male Steller's sea lions are the ones generally seen, either juveniles – who are not yet able to compete in the highly competitive world of the mating beaches – or huge old bulls who have seen better days. The discrepancy in size between the mature and the juvenile males is similar to the one that exists between the males and females. The females are about six to seven feet long, while some of the bulls are up to ten and a half feet long, most of their size visible in their massive forequarters. They waste no effort displaying their vast chests as they loll in the sun on the rocks and roar – just like lions – occasionally chasing off some lesser male who has had the gall to come too close.

Sea lions often stay in the water when the weather is unpleasant, but they seem to love soaking up the sun when it is out. They usually feed after dark – although I've seem them feed during the day – on a variety of fish and shellfish. Humans are not on their list of foods, although a sea lion did take a sizeable chunk out of a man's thigh on the government dock in Ucluelet a couple of years ago. Perhaps my respect for sea lions is overdeveloped, but I am happy to think of them on their rock in the sun as I increase the distance between us.

Behind us, some less menacing marine mammals have been surfacing. Harbour porpoises are fishing about 200 yards from our boats. Adrian has been trying to catch them on film, but they are elusive creatures, shy and quick. From my kayak I have often seen them fishing in pairs. From a motorboat, sightings are less likely. Harbour porpoises are very affected by motorized vessels, nervous of them and flighty when the boats are around. Human development and use of calm waterfront areas has made life difficult for harbour porpoises and, combined with the general decline in fish such as herring, has caused a sharp reduction in their numbers. At one time it was possible to see porpoises in groups of up to 100. Now such sightings are rare. I am always excited when porpoises do appear, grateful for any opportunity to see them. There is something exquisitely graceful in the quick curve of their dark, shiny dorsal fins, as they slick through the water with sureness and purpose.

Harbour porpoises are one of the smallest cetaceans; the largest of them grow to six feet only. Their size is reflected in the diminutive sound of their exhalations. This sound is very different from that of the larger whales. When a grey whale spouts, it sounds like wind blowing down a manhole. It can really make you jump, especially if you are in a kayak. When there is no noise from a motor, even small sounds carry well on the water. On a calm day a grey whale can sound as if it has come up within arm's length of you when, in fact, it is a hundred yards away. Not so with porpoises. Theirs is a quiet little *pffft!* – a piccolo to the grey whale's tuba. On a calm night one September, I listened to harbour porpoises for hours as I lay in my tent at Matleset Narrows, behind Meares Island. They must have fished all night, yet they were still out there in the morning, puffing back and forth across the narrows. The previous day we had seen a group of orcas twice. I remember being surprised at the presence of the porpoises, because orcas do hunt them, slapping their bodies around brutally before devouring them. Perhaps the porpoises thought they were safe, now that the orcas had passed through, or perhaps the fishing was just too good to be missed. Whatever the case, the sound of them spouting nearly always evokes that night for me: the extreme darkness of the sky, the pulsing brightness of the stars, the chill in the air as an autumnal blanket wrapped us in dew. . . .

The porpoises disappear from our realm and we pause while Adrian puts his camera gear safely back into waterproof boxes. We are now close to Vargas again and to the beach that is the source of the roaring surf. I have always referred to this beach as

Paradise Dunes. On the chart it is unnamed and, as with many such places, a variety of names has developed, depending on who visits it or who lives there. I have only landed on this beach once, but I have walked to it several times from the north end of Ahous Beach. The surf that we could hear from Blunden is customary here. Something about the southwestern exposure of the beach and the rise of the sandy ocean floor causes the swell to funnel in. It is rare for conditions to permit landing here. Even paddling close to this area requires caution. The surf will suddenly break further out than usual – a major cause for alarm if it happens to break underneath your kayak. Tumbling through whitewater could have dire consequences, not the least of which is being stranded on a beach so surfy that leaving it is impossible. Still, the sandy faces of the dunes beckon with such allure; fond memories of long walks make me stare wistfully through the surf, wishing I could be there. Suddenly, a roller crests close by us, illustrating the complexity of the area and its inherent dangers. I snap out of the daydream.

Around us the water has become a deep, clear green, its depths concealed by the concise reflections of the clouds painting its surface. We don't have much further to paddle before leaving Vargas Island behind us. We travel easily – a dreamy group – each of us fascinated by the overwhelming sensation of the moment. The crossing, when it comes, is easy. The slow ebb of the tide only becomes noticeable when we near Whaler Islet. As we approach, a slight breeze slices across the water's surface, throwing up small splashes. As we land, the surge slides us sideways and tries to suck us back out again.

It is almost slack tide, that moment of indecision between the ebb and the flood, when little water moves. Slack tide also tends to be a moment of calm, before the weather decides how it is going to behave. I am not too concerned about the breeze that is blowing right now. Once the tide starts to flood, the afternoon's conditions will likely show themselves.

As we remove our stuff from the boats, the wind dies and the conditions start to alternate between cool, cloudy greyness and intense, almost unbearable heat. There seems to be no middle ground. Underfoot, the island is scorching. We hop down the beach like sand fleas, trying to find cool spots for our tender soles, reluctant to put on shoes when there is such deceptively inviting sand around. At lunch we take refuge behind a rock, under some of the trees that so sparsely decorate the island.

Whaler Islet is one of several small islands that hide behind the protective rocky buttresses of Bartlett Island to the south. The collection of rocks and islands here creates the feel of a sudden garden – the watery equivalent of an oasis. But of all the islands, Whaler is surely the most enchanting. Almost all of it is sand. On a hot day in the summer it could be anywhere in the tropics.

There are a few flowers here, mostly Indian paintbrush, its scarlet colour paling now that we have passed the longest day of the year. But the dune grass is verdant – its plump seed-heads wait to open and be scattered; they are lush in comparison to the dryness of the island. Even the trees struggle here, exposed as they are to every zephyr that blows. The desertlike appearance of Whaler is the result of continual shaping and changing by the wind. It is so tempting to camp here, to convince ourselves that we are somewhere tropical, but Whaler is not a place to camp. The slightest change in the weather can transform it from paradise to chaos in seconds flat, leaving you stunned by your lack of foresight. Perhaps the sense of being able to look but not touch is another part of Whaler's attraction.

There are other reasons for the fascination with this island. One story holds that

Flowers out of a stone: blooming stonecrop transforms even the most austere rock surfaces.
At most times of year this plant's colouring is subtle, blending easily
with its usual rocky background.

whales chose to come here when they were dying. In fact, in the last 30 years several whale carcasses have washed up on Whaler. The story makes sense if you consider that when a whale is distressed or in ill health, its desire is to be in calm, shallow water, where it can breathe without effort. However, when they move into shallow water, they can get stranded. As they become progressively weaker, they are less able to move. When the tide goes out, they are left behind.

The water surrounding Whaler is shallow and sandy. It is possible to land anywhere here, and it is usually possible to land on the leeward side, whichever side that happens to be. This feature lured two people here many years ago to investigate the rotting carcass of a grey whale. It was supposed to be the perfect day to check out the whale. The wind was blowing from the southeast, so the duo would be upwind of the unbearable stench all the way from Tofino. And since there was a stiff breeze, it would be possible to examine the whale quite closely, without feeling overly nauseated. But plans that seem foolproof can make for very entertaining stories later. This adventure started well; the two men reached the island without incident and found that they could indeed approach the whale with some degree of tolerance. The whale was in an advanced stage of decay and the odour it would have been giving off would be beyond description. Only those who have been unfortunate enough to smell a whale's carcass can appreciate the overwhelming awfulness of it. These men had encountered the smell before and were taking no chances – they thought.

They had not expected the sudden shift in wind direction that would occur at slack tide that day. Nor had they anticipated being stranded on the now-windward side of the island while their boat lay in the lee side – directly in the path of the scent. They hadn't anticipated the severe nausea they would feel as they made a run for the boat, stopping only to be sick along the way. And they hadn't anticipated that the motor would not start right away, agonizingly delaying their departure. Finally, they hadn't anticipated that they would have to drive home amidst the wafting stink, horribly weak from their adventure but alive, at least, to tell the tale.

We wander around the island feeling like castaways, admiring the 360-degree view. On one side of us, the mountains of Flores Island swoop down to wide, sandy bays. To the northeast is the mainland, with Catface mountain and the white tips of the coast mountains behind. Further east, the hills of Meares, Lone Cone and Mount Colnett show themselves above the white shores of Vargas. It is a privilege to look at so much temperate rainforest that is still old growth, still untouched by modern saws and multinational companies. The soft, many-hued greens indicate the variety of tree species and suggest each area's unique sense of balance. This vista is so big, yet the details of the tiny islands and coves are so varied, so interesting. Few places are this compelling.

On the other side of the island we see a group of kayakers arrive. They tuck themselves behind a sand dune and sweat out their lunch in the hot sun. The island accommodates us all easily. There is no sense of crowding or that the wilderness experience is being diminished. When travellers are sensitive to one another, the journey can flow pretty smoothly. One such instance of courtesy took place at a beach on Vargas. Our group watched in dismay as kayak after kayak pulled up on the sand that evening. Surely it would be like a neighbourhood barbeque. Maybe we should just radio Tofino and order a mass drop-off of pizza and beer in anticipation of a rowdy night. But as quietly as they had arrived, the little groups of people tucked themselves into the beach and the forest; by dusk there was barely a trace of their presence. In contrast, I have had moments when just two people have completely ruined my camping experience with their lack of respect for the surroundings and the people in them.

While my thoughts run in this vein, I am reminded that there is now a company in Tofino offering helicopter tours that include drop-offs to Whaler Islet. Jan and Adrian and I discuss this, finding no shortage of ideas about how we would react to the arrival of a helicopter right now. The very sound of one makes me feel instantly as if I am in a war zone.

The issue of helicopter tours is a touchy one. It's hard to qualify what's obnoxious and what's not, because so much personal bias is involved. The tinny scream of a jet ski is anathema to some, others are oblivious to it; motorboat traffic can be noisy and stressful to kayakers, but kayaks irritate motorboaters who consider them a nuisance. The different ways of experiencing the wilderness do not always sit easily next to one another and so far, in Clayoquot Sound, little thought has been given to the future, with tour companies blossoming like flowers, filling the sound with visitors in a whole-hearted embrace of tourism, an embrace that is, potentially, the kiss of death.

The arrival of a helicopter would definitely not sit well with the way in which we three kayakers are experiencing the wilderness now. We have no difficulty identifying this, but I am sad to think that at some point in the future, the fact of life around here may be the shudder of blades drowning out the soft whoosh of the waves as they surge and retreat against the sand.

This break has been perfect. While we had lunch and explored the island, the tide went out and came back in, so we don't have to heave the boats anywhere. We stuff the red lunch bags back into their crevices and say farewell to this beautiful desert isle. Soon we are moving across Russell Channel towards Flores, with the tide and a light breeze to freshen us up.

Last year the body of water between Vargas and Flores was visited by a humpback whale. For a period of a few weeks, paddling was a nerve-wracking proposition. Humpbacks are larger than grey whales, measuring about 50 feet, with big winglike flippers. They have a reputation for being the most acrobatic of whales. The whale that was here last year seemed to be cruising a particular circuit and moved fairly quickly. One minute it would be a quarter of a mile away; the next minute it would be throwing itself out of the water, uncomfortably close to the boat I was in. Some of the motorboaters began to feel nervous about these sudden, unpredictable and dramatic appearances. The whale was lunge-feeding, a technique specific to humpbacks, whereby the animal plows through food-rich areas with its mouth wide open. The movement culminates in an upward lunge or leap and – hopefully – a healthy mouthful of food.

Another humpback feeding technique occurs when the whale attempts to corral its prey with a lasso of bubbles. The humpback moves underneath the plankton or small fish on which it intends to feed, then it sends up a wall of bubbles, like a curtain or a net. Plankton and other small fish are very sensitive to water turbulence and tend to move away from it. As the humpback travels in a circle, sending up bubbles, its prospective dinner is being rounded up, concentrated in one area so that the whale has only to swoop upwards, jaws wide, in order to engulf a suitably huge mouthful. To make the process even more efficient, the humpback has pleats in its throat that open like an accordion, allowing it to make room for as much food as possible. This impressive method of fishing can be performed by a single whale or by a group of whales. I had never seen a humpback before, and the sight of one lunging made a great impression on me – not the least part of which was having little desire to be in a kayak above the whale at the moment it chose to surface. Being caught by a boomer would surely pale in comparison to being blown out of the water by a 50-foot whale.

For many whale watchers – locals and tourists alike – seeing the humpback whales here last year was a first. A small group of humpbacks usually summers near La Perouse Bank, a shallow area about 30 miles off the coast, but in recent years they haven't spent much time close to land. Once, they were thought to be the most common whale here and were found inshore and offshore, all through the inlets. Although they were harder to catch than grey whales, they were more popular among the Natives because they were bigger, had more baleen and twice the oil, and were supposed to be much tastier. They were more popular among the commercial whalers too, hence their drastic reduction in numbers. In the mid-1900s the local humpback population was hunted to near extinction. By the 1930s there were so few left that whalers had to shift their focus to other species. Humpbacks were killed up to 1966 at Coal Harbour, further up the coast of Vancouver Island. Shortly afterwards the species was granted protection and has been slowly recovering ever since.

The sweeping arm of Ahous Bay, culminating at Ahous Point (bottom left). Some years, this bay is a popular summer feeding ground for resident grey whales.

There is another factor related to the absence of humpbacks. These whales fed heavily on small fish called pilchards (also called Pacific sardines). Pilchards were plentiful in the inlets, so plentiful, in fact, that around 1917 they became the focus of a huge industry. They were caught and canned by the thousands for human consumption. Later the nature of the pilchard industry shifted, and the fish were just boiled down and reduced to oil, for use in paint and margarine and other such oil-based products. This wasteful industry accelerated rapidly; by 1947 there were absolutely no pilchards left. Elders who watched the demise of the pilchard were truly shocked by the rapidity of the extermination. In the space of 30 years a food that Natives had used since time immemorial had been eradicated.

For the handful of whales that remained, an important food source was lost. For those humans who participated in the fishery, an important lesson was demonstrated, although perhaps not learned: humans were capable of wiping out a species by overfishing.

But lately, in what seems like a miraculous turn of events, pilchards have started

This bald eagle seems captivated by the evening light. Bald eagles are common on the West Coast, often visible on the treetop perches from which they survey their domain.

to return to local waters. In fact, throughout British Columbia their numbers have been on the rise, as they spread north from remnant populations elsewhere. Incredibly, there is even a test fishery for the returning pilchards, in place since 1996, to explore the possibility of catching the beleaguered fishies once again.

Since the returning pilchards have not escaped human notice, perhaps the humpbacks have noticed them, too. That they should both return to the same area at the same time, after such a long absence seems too coincidental. But perhaps last year was a fluke; after all, the humpbacks have been less conspicuous this year. Certainly there are none catapulting themselves out of the water right now.

What does catapult out of the water, however, are harbour porpoises. We have crossed most of the open water and the conditions have been fine. Close to our boats several porpoises are fishing – quite aggressively, too – punching up through the water around us. One surfaces right off my bow at a distance of about four feet. It quickly comes up again, this time about 20 feet away. Maybe there are pilchards here after all. A number of birds are also feeding in this location, so I pull out my fishing rod and plop the buzz bomb overboard. It quickly wiggles down out of sight and I spend some time jigging, wondering what the porpoises are getting and what's attracting the birds.

Sometimes when birds gather in a frenzy at the surface, it's possible to see a ball of tiny fish packed tightly together, having been herded upwards by larger fish and diving birds. Once the little fish get into a position like that they don't stand much of a chance. Bigger fish eat them from below, seagulls eat them from above and diving birds swipe at them from the sides. It can be quite a banquet. It doesn't look like there's a concentrated ball of fish here, because the birds are not that excited or that focused. The porpoises, too, are cruising wide transects, gradually moving further away. Still, I'm hopeful. And I'm trying not to think about catching a dogfish. These are often one of the larger fish that push the small ones to the surface, and they are definitely not the kind of fish I would want to catch from my kayak. They are strong and have a habit of thrashing around a lot.

No such fate befalls me. Nothing even nibbles at my lure. Slightly disappointed, I wonder how I'm going to make good on my promise to catch a fish for my omnivorous companions.

All this time we have been gradually drifting towards some rocks near Kutcous

Point on the southeastern shore of Flores Island. Adrian has gone to look for goose-neck barnacles on the rocks. As I paddle that direction, a coho jumps between two rocks in front of me. It must be an omen, I think, so I paddle over and jig in the same place the salmon just jumped. Seconds later I pull up a medium-size kelp greenling, just perfect for feeding three hungry people. Holding it by the side of my boat, I bonk it on the head with the gnarled root of driftwood that I keep on deck specifically for that purpose. It doesn't need much of a death blow, being already exhausted by its journey to the surface. Truth to tell, this fish did not put up much of a fight; in fact, I thought I had hooked up a piece of seaweed and was as surprised about catching the fish as the fish probably was about being caught. But even though this fish is not the small salmon I had in mind, it is perfect. It's the right size, so we won't have to worry about keeping leftovers cool, and its white meat will go deliciously with any meal. On top of that, it responded to my lure, elevating my credibility, which makes me greatly excited. I paddle over to the others to share the happy news, and find that Adrian has also found some seafood. He has picked some goose-neck barnacles − strange, intertidal shellfish that protrude from the rocks on long, scaly necks. We immediately think about heading for shore and making camp, lured on by our taste buds.

Bearing in mind that there may still be some sort of wind from the south, we choose to land on the more northerly of the two beaches on Flores that make up Whitesand Cove. We tuck into a corner behind a smaller island that lies close to shore, in a spot that will allow us to retreat into the forest if the need arises. It is still not clear how much we are likely to be affected by the weather, but without any access to the forest, Whitesands is not the best place to be in a storm.

Once again we arrive near sunset, having blissfully dallied along our way. After the usual gear-hauling ceremony, we start a fire for baking the fish. On Blunden there was no need to protect our food from bears − mice and crows were the more likely problem. Tonight we will need to be aware of black bears. We are within range of Ahousaht, where there is a garbage dump. Not only are there bears in the vicinity, those bears may be habituated to human food.

Food caches are a necessary evil on camping trips. It is so important to be self-contained, to keep a tidy camp and not leave out food, to minimize traces of our presence, to keep the sight, sound and smell of humans away from the creatures whose territory this is. But rigging up a food cache is a lot of extra work. Much depends on finding a suitable tree, with a perfect branch hanging out over the beach, capable of bearing the weight of a week's worth of food. As well as being strong, the branch has to be high enough to pull the food a serious distance in the air, but not so high that it is impossible to throw a rope over it. Then, last thing at night, when tiredness has settled over everyone and the tents beckon invitingly, you have to zip that last tube of toothpaste into the duffel bag, haul it down the beach (stumbling over tree roots that were impossible to see in the beam of the flashlight), seek out the correct piece of rope, tie the correct knot and coordinate the required number of people to heave in the required directions. There is no point in making a food cache if it's not going to be done right, however, and the extra effort brings the reward of a job well done plus the confidence of a good night's sleep. I'm thankful to find a perfect tree on this beach and the job of setting up the ropes goes smoothly.

There is still much to do, so I take the sacrificial fish down to the water's edge to clean it. Cleaning fish feels like such an important act. It may sound illogical, but when I am cleaning a fish I feel as if this is the best moment to show my appreciation for it, even though I am about to disembowel it. But there are situations to which logic cannot be applied; it's late and the day has been long. Whatever illogic there is fails to bother me as I perform the dual acts of thanking and gutting the fish. I leave the innards high on a rock for the ravens, reasoning that this is a natural source of food, not something that will cause problems between humans and animals further down the line. I wrap the rest of the fish in tinfoil, adding the large shell of a horse clam as extra protection against the heat.

Looking up I see a dark band of fog beetling towards us. As forecast, the wind is coming from the south, pushing the low, vapoury cloud along with it. The fog seems to be extending tentacles; it is moving fast, blotting out everything. Five minutes ago I could see the islands at the far end of the cove. Now I can't. It's going to be here any moment.

Oddly, the fog bypasses our section of the beach and rolls over the kayaks at the far end. This respite is unlikely to be long lived, but the whole performance has been spectacular. Suddenly, the lower part of our view is obscured; the top half is still perfectly visible. Catface, Lone Cone and Mount Colnett beam out over the grey cloud beneath them, beautifully lit by the lowering sun.

The speed at which the fog has just eradicated the landscape perfectly illustrates the conditions in which accidents happen on the coast. Fog can be one of the most lethal weather effects on the water. Dealing with it requires not only solid navigational skills, but courage. Travelling in fog with only a compass for reference means trusting yourself – your own choice of bearing and your skill at following the compass. In the fog, time passes slowly. Minutes seem like hours. Without a watch to keep track, it's impossible to gauge how long travelling the route takes or how close the shore is. It's therefore important to know the average travelling speed of the group and to be able to estimate the strength of the wind and the tide, and to factor those things in. Once a plan is established, it must be adhered to. Only if something is obviously wrong should the route be reconsidered, for instance, if a known landform appears, proving that you've made an error.

Another characteristic of fog is the way it carries sound – in some cases, amplifying it. Faraway surf can seem close, as can motorboats. This deceptive quality is one of the most challenging aspects of dealing with fog. In fog it is hard to judge the accuracy of the senses, which can make it hard to trust oneself. This can contribute to fear and lead to panic. The only thing left to trust, then, is the compass, the bearing and

Fog softens the edges of this driftlog at Whitesand Cove, Flores Island. Moments earlier, the same log had been bathed in evening sunlight. When a bank of fog rolls in, the speed of its approach is astonishing.

the watch. Needless to say, it is better to avoid travelling in fog, but one should always be prepared for it.

The risk of sudden fog is another reason to minimize the length of open-water crossings, and not just because of the chance of getting lost. In Clayoquot Sound the growing number of high-speed charter boats is increasing the likelihood of marine collisions. Many boats now have Global Positioning Systems (GPS), which can tell drivers where they are to within a hundred feet. These units make it possible for drivers to travel fast, in reduced visibility, without worrying about getting lost. But Coast Guard regulations state that motor-powered boats should travel "at a safe speed adapted to the conditions." The regulations include taking into consideration the limitations of navigational equipment and "the possibility that small vessels . . . and other floating objects may not be detected by radar at an adequate range." These rules are not always followed. Crossing open water in thick fog in a kayak entails relying on chance to avoid a horrible collision. Having come close to being run over on one occasion, I know the feeling of helplessness. Now it is rare for me to travel in fog deliberately. Only if the route sticks close to the shoreline or passes over water too shallow for motorboats will I consider it. The risks are just too great.

So our lovely day of sunshine has ended in a damp grey cloud. It's amazing how easy it is to forget about fog. In the middle of winter, my memory conjures up only the most flawless summer weather, conveniently forgetting the countless number of foggy days that can make the summer a disappointment. Sometimes it is possible to see the sun through the fog, to know that blue sky is just a hundred feet away. Oh, how tantalizing this is to sodden coastal dwellers, to whom the sight of sun is precious.

Interestingly, the same northwesterly wind that brings nice weather also creates fog. Although this wind brings the high pressure systems and sunshine, it blows across the land onto the water, gradually pushing warm surface water away from the coast. Equally gradually, this warm water is replaced by cooler water that comes up from the deep, in a process known as upwelling. The northwesterly that pushes warm water away is itself warm, moist wind. When it mingles with the cold upwelling it has created, the by-product is fog.

On the coast, in the daytime, cool ocean air is attracted to the heat of the land. The heat rises. At night the process reverses as the land cools. Fog often forms at night, dissipating in the heat of the day, once the onshore breeze pattern is established. Eventually, however, the fog bank gets so big that it only burns off for a few hours in the afternoon. Sometimes it seems as if it is never going to go away. It may even create its own little low-pressure system that can involve a day of rain. After that the weather will improve for a while, but as soon as the northwesterly starts blowing, you can be sure it won't be long before there's fog again.

On the plus side, the visible special effects of fog can be unparalleled. Illusions come and go; a single island will shine brilliantly – blue sky above and blue water below – the only thing distinguishable in an otherwise featureless cloud; a view will appear or disappear in seconds; mist will wrap itself around the treetops, wafting spectral fancies above and through the forest.

The moisture that fog brings is important too, accounting for up to 35 percent of the annual precipitation in Clayoquot Sound at a time of year when not much rain usually falls. This summer there has been no shortage of rain, however, and it is depressing when the fog arrives after only two and a half days of sunshine. I make a point of recalibrating my hearty pessimism about the weather, having let it slide slightly during the sunnier moments of the day.

After setting up the tent we collect some small pieces of wood to add to the fire. As well as the fish there are slices of potatoes and yams, drizzled with olive oil and fresh herbs, that also need to be baked. The fire has to be kept at a fairly even heat – hot, but not raging – which means that it will need constant tending. There is no shortage of driftwood here. The trick lies in finding the best pieces, pieces that will burn instead of smouldering, but that will also last a while and not have to be constantly replaced. What is also important is taking only that which will be used. There's nothing worse than showing up at a beach and finding huge, half-charred logs and a dirty black patch of coals just where you want to set up your tent. Ideally, I like to burn everything down to ashes and even dispose of the ash pile. A small fire can provide all the comforts of a larger one, with none of the drawbacks. Small fires are more sociable too; the group gathers more closely around them.

We have a small fire tonight, and since we are all ravenously hungry and our food is actually in the fire producing wonderful smells, it is not surprising that we are gathered here.

And it is truly a feast. We eat and talk late into the night. The bones of the fish are picked clean in the manner of true appreciation. The scaly skins of the steamed gooseneck barnacles are peeled away to reveal delicious sections of pink-orange muscle. Ginger tea and organic dark chocolate enhance the glow of smug satisfaction that must surely be visible from far away. As the fire is reduced to coals our voices wander out softly into the moist darkness.

The mood is only mildly interrupted by the need to clean up and cache the food. Everything happens fluidly and the sight of the sleeping bags is as welcome as everything else that has taken place today. The trip has really begun to take on a life of its own and the fact that our other lives feel so far away is wonderful. It means that there is now more freedom for us to immerse ourselves in the journey.

Chapter Four
LANDBOUND

*Along the Ahousaht Wild Side Heritage Trail,
south from Whitesand Cove*

WHEN I STUMBLE BLEARILY OUT OF THE TENT IN THE morning, I find that last night's fog has metamorphosed into a damp uniform greyness. Since today is supposed to be a day off from kayaking, I have no qualms about crawling back into my sleeping bag for a little while. Certainly there have been no signs of life from the other sleeping bags; in fact, the only sign of life right now is the group of crows feeding quietly on the beach. It seems odd to see crows behaving peacefully. I'm so used to protecting my groceries from them that I seem to have forgotten that they have nonhuman feeding habits as well. I don't know exactly what they are getting, but they are digging in the sand with great diligence. I snuggle back into the warmth of the sleeping bag and doze, until a clamour of personal guilt drags me outside. The feeling must be a by-product of guiding: should I not have poured the clients their coffee by now? Shouldn't the fruit be sliced up and the French toast be toasting?

There is a slight drizzle, so Jan and I put up a tarp over the area we have been

*Sunset at Kutcous Point, Flores Island. A rugged section of coast looks deceptively
peaceful as the moment of calm descends, however temporarily, along with the sun on
its journey beyond the horizon.*

using to prepare food. As I pour a cup of tea, I look up and see a squatting cloud racing towards us from Bartlett Island, obviously full of wetness. Thankful for the tarp, we put away anything that shouldn't get wet and pull on some more warm clothes.

As the cloud approaches we watch this replay of last night's fog, and count down to the moment when the rain will start. Satisfied that we don't need to rush anywhere, I pull out the food bag and start mixing a batch of apple pancakes, mentally rebuking myself for not having packed a better frying pan. The silly little pieces of stainless steel that these days, in outdoor shops, are called frying pans are absolutely useless. I know this, so why did I bring one along? Making pancakes with camping stoves that have no simmer setting and frying pans that don't deserve to be called frying pans is frustrating beyond belief. Eventually I get a system figured out. Each panful is able to survive four seconds on the heat and four seconds off. And the pancakes are delicious, which more than compensates for the dreary morning and the rain.

We turn on the VHF radio and listen to the marine weather forecast in the vague hope that there will be some good news. Even though we are not intending to travel on the water today, it would be helpful to have an idea of what lies in store for us. Listening to the VHF has become an integral part of any morning's routine. At one time I used to pay attention to the forecast only when I was guiding, preferring to trust my instincts when travelling on my own. It was not until I paddled in Kyuquot Sound with a friend one October that I discovered that the marine weather forecast could occasionally provide some very important information.

It was the second day of this particular trip. The first day we had covered a distance of about 20 miles, from our launching spot part of the way up the Artlish River inlet to Spring Island on the exposed western coast of the mainland. Our plan was to explore Spring Island for a day or two, before continuing up the coast to Checleset Bay – home of the sea otters. It was late in the year, but so far the weather had held up. At the very end of the first day we hauled the boats up a steep shell beach just before darkness fell. The next morning we decided to move camp to a neck of land that was visible from the beach we were on. It offered shelter from both the northwesterly and the southeasterly winds and had small protected beaches on either side. The chart showed that the area was also close to a trail that crossed Spring Island to the more protected east side. This was not going to be an ambitious journey; we had dispensed with ambition the day before.

So we lazed around on the beach, built a fire, made pancakes and relaxed in the extreme softness of the morning. It was a beautiful day and we weren't going very far. Listening to the weather forecast seemed like a waste of precious batteries. But we listened anyway. Our ears pricked up at the words "Pan-Pan." Sometimes this phrase precedes an announcement about marine hazards, sometimes there's a boat in distress or a person lost, only rarely is there a tsunami.

But sure enough, on this occasion, an earthquake in Japan had initiated a tsunami – a tidal wave – which was expected to reach the B.C. coast at 3:30 p.m. Small, cold stones slid down my throat to settle on top of the pancakes in my stomach. We looked at each other in horror. We were on a completely flat island, as far offshore as possible, and it was now eleven o'clock. If the report was accurate, we had four and a half hours in which to pack up the boats and paddle to somewhere that had at least one contour line. We decided to head to the village of Kyuquot, about five miles to the northeast. Surely Kyuquot would have a preplanned, safe place for escaping tsunamis? We estimated that the trip, including the time it would take us to squeeze two weeks' worth of food back into the boats, would only take about two and a half hours; we hoped to be in Kyuquot by 1:30 p.m. Perhaps I have packed a boat faster in my life, but it's unlikely.

The paddle across was not uneventful. Was it the earthquake that caused the swell to rise so dramatically? Already pumped with adrenaline, we paddled hard and watched the rolling swell as it crested thunderously over invisible rocks. We dodged whitewater and ducked through gaps in surf breaks. Not until we reached the islands in the lee of Spring Island and to the northeast did the conditions become more manageable. Then, just as we were passing a small, inhabited island, a man on shore began waving his arms at us frantically, in the traditional signal of distress. We debated whether he just wanted to tell us about the tsunami or he actually needed help, but a distress signal is a distress signal, so we paddled over to see him.

"There's a tsunami should be here in a few hours," the man informed us when we finally arrived. "You shouldn't be on the water."

We told him our plans and he nodded. "Probably won't amount to much anyway," he sighed. "Last one just made the tide run faster. Was like a river through here." He gestured at the narrow passageway we had just come through. "A few boats got sunk; that was about all."

It was interesting to hear about the effects of tsunamis past, and we could have stayed there chatting all day had we not been a little preoccupied with the effects of tsunamis future, and with the time of our arrival in Kyuquot. We paddled on, thanking the man, wondering if tsunamis ever arrived earlier than predicted.

A few minutes later a helicopter buzzed by, returning to circle overhead. Crouching above us, making wind and waves and noise, the helicopter proceeded to impart some information. If the helicopter crew were telling us about the tsunami, however, we were lucky that we already knew, because whatever came over the loudspeaker was completely unintelligible. Listening to it was a total waste of time. On top of that, the helicopter was making it hard for us to paddle. We ignored it and continued, deciding not to get stiff necks from peering skywards. It wasn't as if we could lip-read information from a helicopter, anyway.

Our journey was delayed by a few more such helpful warnings from people in motorboats, until we finally entered the harbour of Kyuquot with, luckily, 45 minutes to spare. Kyuquot is a community of people whose lives revolve so completely around the water that almost anyone would be likely to know where we should go and – we hoped – what we should do with our boats. We had not anticipated the total absence of human life that greeted us. It was like entering a ghost town: no kids, no grandparents – not even any dogs. Even the general store was closed. Everyone had been evacuated already. But to where? Slightly bewildered, we stood on the government dock and used the pay phone to call Tofino and update friends as to our whereabouts.

It was while we were calling that a couple of people emerged from a huge seine boat at the dock. They asked us what we were doing and we asked them what we should be doing. They told us that they were planning on protecting their boat by going out to sea when it was time to do so. In deep water, the effects of a tsunami are much diminished. We jumped at the offer to join them – kayaks and all.

Suddenly, we found ourselves cozily seated on a plush couch in a luxurious boat, being fed muffins and tea, watching the latest tsunami forecasts on a colour TV. The estimated height of the wave grew smaller every 10 minutes. By the time 3:30 p.m. rolled around, we were back at the dock, casually standing around and leaning over its edge, hoping for action, our fears temporarily allayed. That was when the tsunami was cancelled.

Two hours of paddling brought us to the beach for which we had been aiming that morning; we had travelled at least 10 miles to get there and encountered taxing conditions in certain places. We whipped out the tarp and the tents and cooked supper in the quickening October dusk. What a day, we thought. To round off the night and improve our sleep, we decided to listen to the forecast again, just to make sure nothing else was on its way.

And once more our ears pricked up at the words, "Pan-Pan."

No! It can't be . . . not another one. . . . The cold stones resurfaced in my gut as we listened intently to the radio. Our minds were racing. It was too late to paddle to Kyuquot now; it would be impossible to deal with the swell in this darkness.

Then: ". . . is expected to reach the coast at 15:30. . . ."

We cursed the broadcasters roundly that night, for playing the same warning all day, for not reporting the official cancellation. But I always listen to the VHF on trips now, no matter how short a trip I am planning. As well, whenever I eat pancakes I think about tsunamis.

And so our day on Flores begins with some tsunami pancakes and the weather. I am thankful the forecast is optimistic, calling for some clearing in the afternoon — perfect for the walk we have in mind.

The traveller's eleventh commandment: relax often and enjoy what lies around you.
When the sun is out, good resting spots beckon; in this case, the sand dunes near
Kutcous point. And what better place for a nap?

Whitesand Cove is situated along the newly built Ahousaht Wild Side Heritage Trail, which links a string of beaches from the village of Ahousaht to Cow Bay. The trail has been also blazed up to the top of Mount Flores, although apparently this section is rougher than the sections linking the beaches. This trail was built with funds provided by the Western Canada Wilderness Committee, but the idea for it came from a group of about a dozen women in Ahousaht, who wished to tap into the growing tourism industry in Clayoquot Sound and to provide a guided hiking service along the spectacular outer coast. The Walk on the Wild Side, as it is called, is not confined to hiking; cultural history is explained by the guides and there is also the option of a traditional salmon barbeque. Had the departure date for this trip been more certain, we could have arranged for one of these tours. The way things have worked out, however, we will have to make do with our own observations and the newly published guidebook to the trail. This book, a collection of stories by the Ahousaht elder Stanley Sam, elaborates on the informative hand-painted signs posted at historically significant locations along the route. It's a shame that we will not have any verbal commentary to round out the written information. Next time I will be sure to arrange a tour, but with this weather, perhaps not having one is just as well; we are unlikely to cover any great distance today and we need to be back on the water again tomorrow.

When the rain tapers off a bit I wander down the beach to the sand dunes at the far end. Sand dunes are delicate microenvironments, often home to plant species that may not be common anywhere else. I take an identification book with me in the hopes of improving my repertoire of plant knowledge.

Along the way, I find myself following the tracks of a wolf. The first thing we noticed on arriving at this beach was the quantity of wolf-paw prints. Gauging the number of wolves in Clayoquot Sound is hard, because they frequent different areas at different times of year. They are also among the most elusive of wild mammals, appearing before humans rarely, if at all. For a while, there appeared to be few – if any – wolves on Flores. It was rumoured that an entire pack had been shot while they were swimming from one island to another. This rumour appalls me. The reality is that a fear of wolves is instilled in human beings at an early age. Innocuous fairy tales about big bad wolves can have surprisingly long-lived effects. Attitudes built on fear still prevail, usually quite close to the surface.

The conflict between attitudes of acceptance and attitudes based on fear became apparent over the winter, when wolves were seen on several occasions in Tofino, known culprits in the killings of several dogs. Inevitably, there was an outcry from people who wanted the wolves deported. The wolves were likely the same ones that had lived in the Long Beach area for years and had beaten up dogs in the communities of Esowista and Opitsaht on several occasions. However, when the wolves moved outside the non-native community – their habits going with them – they quickly became seen as a problem. The wolves have not been known to attack humans. Their attacks on dogs may be related to an issue of dominance, but this winter's unusually high snowfall meant that food was scarce for the wolves. They may have found domestic animals to be a useful stop-gap measure. Certainly, as soon as the summer rolled around, they disappeared.

I am excited to see the wolf tracks here, although all of them seem to have been left by the same lone wolf on its regular patrol. There is a distinctive mark that accompanies every set of prints that indicates that the animal may be dragging one

The intense yellow of the dune grass highlights these sand dunes at Kutcous Point.
Be cautious, though: the coarse blades can graze bare legs with their prickly edges.

*Keeping tracks: have we been following this wolf? Or has it been following us? This particular wolf
has one lazy foot that leaves a slight drag mark in the sand with every step,
making it easy to trace the tracks to the same individual.*

foot. A friend who has seen this particular wolf was surprised that it did not appear to limp, despite the drag marks that it leaves behind.

Along with the wolf tracks on this beach is a scattering of shells and rocks. Grades of fine dark sand at the top of the beach become speckled white closer to shore and dark grey at the water. A loose collection of small white clamshells lies halfway along the beach, studded with the occasional moonsnail shell. I continue towards the sand dunes at the north end, encountering a fox sparrow parent along the way. The nest is obviously situated in the thicket of alder across from the sparrow's perch, close to one of historical signs of the Wild Side trail.

The story that is related about this site is that a man once saw two sea serpents sliding down the sand dunes into the sea here. Sea serpents comprise an important part of Nuu-chah-nulth spiritual history and stories about them are still related often. In this particular story, the man was said to have discovered impressions in the sand where the sea serpents had been lying, as well as some of their scales.

I check the sand for any signs of recent occupation before settling in to examine the variety of flowers around me. Most noticeable is the beach morning glory, with

The silvery heads of the beach carrot (Glehnia littoralis), also known as beach silver-top, sprawl gracefully over a sand dune at Whitesand Cove, Flores Island. Sand dunes are fragile environments, easily disturbed by the feet of careless walkers.

its delicate pink and white petals and its distinctive, trumpetlike, morning glory shape. Splashes of yellow come from the yellow sand-verbena and the dune tansy (the Haida name for which translates as "sloppy yellow beach leaves"). Here and there, sharp-looking clumps of big-headed sedge contrast with the soft silver hairs of beach carrot flower heads. Beach sorrel pokes up conspicuously amidst the thick green carpet of kinnikinnick that has spread abundantly over the sandy slopes. This tongue-twisting name is supposed to have derived from the Algonkin language and refers to the use of the plant for smoking. Several coastal Native groups, including the Nuu-chah-nulth, also dried the leaves and smoked them. The plant has powerful medicinal uses as well, as a diuretic and for curing infections of the kidneys and the bladder.

Several years ago I was overcome by curiosity about kinnikinnick as a form of tobacco. I dried a small bag of the leaves and later tried to smoke them. At first I thought that the mixture had not ignited. There was no feeling in my throat. Then I noticed a huge cloud of smoke coming out of my mouth and nose. Shocked, I jumped up to see if my clothes had caught fire, but it was merely the nature of the tobacco – mild and very smoky. Needless to say, the experiment was short-lived. It was unnerving to feel so much like a dragon.

Looking east from Whitesand Cove, this fishing boat heads out to sea with Catface Mountain in the background. It may have come from the nearby village of Ahousaht, which offers a quiet, protected harbour.

Around me the sky is still heavy and grey, but an intense glare makes the water difficult to rest my eyes on. I hope the glare is a precursor to the clearing that is supposed to take place later on. There is still a damp chill in the air, however, and I have grown quite stiff by sitting in the sand enjoying the surroundings. There is something about the sweep of the dunes and the backdrop of Catface and Meares that holds my gaze.

Each of us has been up to our own devices this morning, which is good. The need to do things on your own can get neglected on trips, but should be an instituted part of the plan. On some trips the group dynamic can be so strong that the travellers spend all their time experiencing each other, never really going beyond that to a deeper interaction with their environment. Rainy days are often the perfect excuse to take time out and ensure that each person has a measure of solitude, so that this is not found wanting later on.

I wander slowly back to camp along the water's edge, still feeling the chill of inactivity. Rather than pack a lunch to take with us on the trail this afternoon, Jan and I decide to take a break from the regular lunchtime fare and brew something warming – curried lentils with a soupçon of sea asparagus. All the cooking equipment is still out from breakfast, but we will have to put it away after preparing lunch, and hang up the food again before leaving. We start tidying up odds and ends, making sure that there is nothing the wind can blow away, nothing that will attract crows or bears, nothing that will attract curious humans, either. Unfortunately, thievery does exist in the wilderness, much as it would be nice to presume otherwise. Things left lying around can encourage this kind of light-fingered behaviour. It's easier to zip everything away in a tent and leave the camp looking bare.

By the time we do leave camp we are raring to go. Jan and I have relatively small packs, but Adrian is decorated with a plethora of camera bags and other accessories, none of which seem to hinder him in the least. We head down the beach to the markers at the southwestern end, intending to walk as far as Kutcous Point, maybe further. The trail runs along the shoreline from Ahousaht to Mount Flores; we are going to access it from the midsection. The trail is well identified with colourful Styrofoam floats, the type used to mark crab traps. These are one of the most common items of jetsam on any beach.

Having been out in the open for a while, we find our sudden immersion in the forest a pleasure. Despite the green canopy, there is a feeling of openness here. Bright ferns make up the majority of the undergrowth. The forest floor feels like a velvet display case for the magnificent spruce trees through which we are wandering. In one place, an incredibly tall, slender hemlock has fallen over against a spruce, but has continued to grow upwards in an impressive arc. We stare with open mouths, wondering how much longer it can continue to defy gravity.

Shafts of sun suddenly pierce the lush underworld; the sky must be clearing. All along the trail we marvel at this and that, amazed by the fact that when we were on the beach all this was concealed from us. The environments of beach and forest are so vastly different, but exist so closely together. The transition from one to the other is so brief, almost shocking: exposure – concealment; noise – silence; dryness – dampness.

The trail dips down to the beach and we encounter another sign. We note with interest the care with which these signs have been created. The designs have all been hand-painted by Hutch Sam, Stanley Sam's son, with the lettering done by Stanley's stepson, Harold Lucas. The wooden boards have been beautifully sanded and well varnished against the weather. Not only that, they have been further protected by little hand-split, cedar-shake roofs. These signs are intended to be here for a long time. They are certainly a welcome change from the standard trailside markers that one sees in so many places.

A glance at the guidebook shows that we are at *kwaatswiis* (site number five). The story here is of the awakening of a young man to his powers as a shaman. According to Stanley Sam, the young man went on to become one of the most renowned shamans on the coast, most noted for his visions, which included being able to see things over long distances.

We break out onto the beach to find that the breeze has picked up and the clouds have started to lift. Our mood is equally buoyant, the energy from lunch still apparent in our springy gait. Along this section of the beach there are a number of moonsnail shells and we pick them up excitedly, comparing the different sizes and colours. Findings like this always tempt me to fill my pockets. On one trip, the objects of my desire were some beautifully smooth rocks. Unfortunately, it was a hiking trip and my backpack was already extremely heavy. Goaded by some stubborn instinct, I persisted in taking my treasures, sweating double on the elevation gains and ruining my knees on the descents. An unusually long recovery period ensued. I have

A tapestry of this tree's life lies weathered – exposed. It seems strange that such a root mass never managed to penetrate more deeply into the substrate. Instead it curls its fingers around small rocks and organic matter at the surface.

since learned that it is better to "leave things where they lie," whatever that is a metaphor for. On this beach it would take only few people stuffing their pockets for all trace of these shells to be removed, denying other people the pleasure of discovering them. In the tropics, many beaches that were once littered with shells are now bare, their previous bounty adorning the shelves of travellers worldwide. Difficult as it may be, it is best for us to leave these shells here. Besides, if we do, we will be able to discover them anew on our return.

As it turns out, the shells have distracted us from the next trail entrance; we miss it and end up walking across the reserve land near Kutcous Point. We find ourselves on a more exposed, sandy beach and encounter two canoeists who appear to be in desperate need of people to talk to. And since we are the only people on the beach, we naturally become involved, innocently unprepared for the stream of words that pours out at us. My mind is unable to process all the noise; instead, it follows its own leaves of thought, completely floating away. . . . The sand is so soft here, embedded with white shells. There are more dunes and a patch of stunningly blue lupines. The beach is dotted with massive tree roots, like giant cartwheels, intricately woven. I

The swirling lines of the moonsnail, awash with light and colour. The spiral patterns of these shells evoke thoughts of ancient fossils, prodding the imagination toward visions of long-ago times.

wonder what became of the trunks of these trees, so cleanly sawed off. Did they really become telephone directories? My mind refuses to accept the fact.

After the longish diversion, we resume walking, and find ourselves still following the prints of the wolf. We laugh in recognition, feeling as if we know this wolf, this wolf with the lazy foot that scrapes the beach with every step. In one place we see a track that is obviously very fresh. It was pressed into the sand after this morning's high tide retreated.

Somehow back on track we head for the next trail entrance, again well marked by a crab trap. We must have missed one section of the trail, but have found our way again, thanks to the markers. What becomes clear is that we are now walking on a trail that is quite old. The path has become embedded in the forest floor through years of passing feet, both human and animal. On either side of it lies a profusion of false lily of the valley, its glossy heart-shaped leaves carpeting the soil, providing a perfect background for the display of small white flowers. The sheer quantity of broken clamshells suggests that it is midden soil. If so, this must have been a substantial village site. Before the war with the Ahousaht, this village would have been on O-tsus-aht territory. There is a strong presence here, a flow of sensation that issues out from the trees, raising the hairs on my arms. Everywhere there is sunlight and greenness. We laugh at the collection of superlatives that pour out of our mouths. It is hard to move on, but moving on is part of any journey. And there is always the possibility of even more remarkable discoveries ahead.

Further along the path there is a small cabin made of hand-split cedar boards, surrounded by an overgrowth of thimbleberry bushes and old, bent crabapple trees. A sign on the cabin says: PLEASE RESPECT. FOR EMERGENCY USE ONLY. Inside, it is clean and tidy, with no evidence of mice. This cabin was built at some point after the national park evicted everyone who had been living on Long Beach. At that time, a number of people moved to places where they could maintain independent wilderness lifestyles. Some were able to endure the hardships; others came and went. This cabin has seen many occupants, including Adrian, who once lived here for a short while.

There is no doubt that this land has a magnetic draw for certain people. Living remotely is not easy, but for some, the rewards are greater than the disadvantages. People who have subsisted out in the sound since the 1970s have done so in a scrupulously tidy and self-contained manner, often making everything from scratch, using only the wood on the beaches. Over the years, their tiny dwellings have blended seamlessly into their surroundings. The buildings epitomize a unique, human tribute to beauty, tenacity and respect for the land. In a sense, they have become part of the heritage of the West Coast. There have been homesteaders here for many years and they have always constituted a vibrant part of the local history.

The fact that some of these homesteaders are now being evicted distresses me. Protection of precious areas from logging, which includes designating certain areas as parks, is the reason for the evictions. In 1993 the provincial government announced a decision that was commonly referred to as "The Clayoquot Compromise." The decision allowed logging to continue and, at the same time, created a patchwork of small, provincial parks along the fringes of tourist corridors. In Clayoquot Sound, decisions about these areas include pinning up eviction posters at the half-dozen or so cabins on Vargas and Flores Islands.

Park officials consider themselves lenient, having allowed these people to continue living on this land for several years already. But the homes are so well established, have been here for so many years, are so much a part of the landscape; eviction of these people will surely destroy something irreplaceable.

Must parks necessarily be empty of human inhabitants? The small abandoned cabin we have passed adds colour to an otherwise black-and-white notion about the area's recent history. But that colour could be so much more vivid if there were life here, if people actually lived here – not as tourist attractions, but as a normal part of the landscape. In the context of maintaining the heritage of an area, surely it would be gracious to allow these few homesteaders to stay on. In the Canada of the new century, few other examples of the ways in which it is possible to live lightly on the land will exist.

Perhaps there is an alternative to the standard formula for park operations. There is certainly much room for discussion on the topic. For instance, I have always admired the tenets of the Meares Island Tribal Park, as declared in 1984. The essence of the declaration was to protect the existing ways in which the Tla-o-qui-aht used Meares Island, while at the same time recognizing the needs of non-Natives who want to use the area for recreational purposes and as source of drinking water. The declaration said that, other than water, no resources were to be removed from the island. Since 1984, Natives and non-Natives alike have continued to use the island,

and a sentiment of respect has prevailed. Given a loose framework with which most people can identify, little energy has been needed to uphold the declaration. There is little sign that the land has been abused and there is a widespread feeling of community loyalty to the island.

The Meares Island Tribal Park declaration may not transfer easily to other places. What is interesting about Meares Island is the common acceptance of the land as traditional territory. All other parks in Clayoquot Sound exist on traditional lands, but do not exist at the instigation of the Natives. It will be interesting to see what happens if the Nuu-chah-nulth land question currently under negotiation ever gets resolved. Meanwhile, following the human need for defining and allocating areas, park officials will no doubt carry on administering these areas with their traditional mandate.

Having played the devil's advocate, I must say that, if forced to choose, I would naturally take a park over a clearcut any day; today, this place that is now a park has provided the setting for some wonderful moments of exploration. Pushing through the abundant growth of thimbleberries, we break out onto another expanse of beach, where we are hit by a strong blast of wind. The sun has come out and the sky above us is blue, but over in the west there is still a layer of grey. The combination of wind and open space provokes a surge of friskiness. Jan and I canter across the sand to a rocky headland and climb up it, picking our way through dense, low vegetation. This brutally exposed rock is thick with the most beautifully scented roses. There is clover here, too, and nodding onions. I even find a wild strawberry. Exactly how these plants thrive in such Spartan surroundings is a mystery we happily take at face value. At this moment, the question doesn't really seem to matter. We settle ourselves into the miniature jungle to admire the spectacular view. It is now late in the day and we need to turn back soon. The tide has been coming in and we have a section of creek to cross. Our crossing will be easier if we manage to return to the creek before it becomes a surging mass of waves and current.

After our senses have been filled to the brim by the landscape, we start heading back, once again overwhelmed by the age and serenity of the trail. We can't help but feel privileged to have spent time here, but our decision to return is a good one. Already the water level of the creek has risen quite noticeably and we have to divest ourselves of some of our clothes in order to get across. Since we did not have a swim yesterday, this is actually a good opportunity to bathe, if only briefly. When the hurdle of the creek crossing has been dispensed with, our new goal is to be back in camp before dark. We find the next marker and wiggle through the forest on a section of trail that is not as easy going as the other parts we have used, but it still turns out to be much quicker than the route we took earlier on in the day — probably because we have avoided the section of beach with the talkative campers.

As evening falls, the flutey spirals of birdsong lead us on from one place to another. Once again the voices of the Swainson's thrushes encapsulate the magic of the day and accompany us gently along the homeward path.

The walk back to camp actually goes more quickly than we had anticipated, so there is time enough for me to try my luck at fishing again. It would certainly feel good to contribute fresh food to the menu, although we have eaten incredibly well so far and I am not worried about running out of dinner ingredients. Instead, what I have underestimated is the group's need for sugar. The trail mix has almost run out and I am reluctant to use the expensive after-dinner chocolate during the day; I can

Exhilarated by the wind, we gaze to the southwest as Flores Island and the Garrard Group sprawl away from us. These waters are not hospitable for sea kayakers; the area is best left untravelled for those without the benefit of strong skills and experience.

see that some other form of stop-gap food is going to be necessary. Perhaps we will take a small detour through Ahousaht along our way tomorrow.

After paddling a fully loaded kayak for a few days, it is novel to be going fishing in one that is only carrying safety gear. The sensation is similar that of casting off a 50-pound backpack and then feeling so free that you want to hop, skip and jump. I push off from the beach and head out towards the rocks at Kutcous, thinking that it won't take very long to get to the place where I caught the fish yesterday. I am wrong, perhaps misled by the ease of paddling such a light boat. In fact, the tide is coming in strongly and the wind is in my face.

Fishing does not turn out to be easy, either. It is difficult to remain in one place because of the speedy current. The chop, too, breaks over my bow and makes it hard to focus on jigging. I look around for a nice piece of kelp to tie onto, but the only bits that I can see are too much a part of a general kelp bed and I don't want to fish so close to the kelp that I risk tangling the lure. Sometimes kelp beds are excellent places to catch fish. They are like underwater forests, and protect smaller fish from strong currents and larger fish. In a way, they are like nurseries, but although they offer protection they are not a guarantee against being eaten. The kelp beds themselves attract their fair share of predators – myself among them.

I do battle with the wind and the tide and the fishing lure. Then, just when everything begins to go smoothly, I hook onto something stationary – probably a rock – and while I am freeing the line, the hook bends. When I try to straighten it, it breaks. Good hook! So, then, I am left tying on a new lure while the wind and tide buffet the boat and whisk me out past the rocks into deeper water. I begin to think that I am trying too hard, that this venture was not destined for success. But since I have now tied on a brand-new "spinning minnow" I feel obliged to try it out. For some reason I don't trust this lure, perhaps because I bought it in a camping shop, not the kind of place I would usually buy fishing gear. Besides, it is fluorescent pink. Although my buzz bomb was fluorescent green, the green seemed more natural. Pink does not fit my image of what constitutes an attractive dinner morsel for a cod. I am not an expert, however, and taste buds are my only motivator as far as fishing is concerned.

I can't stick with the fishing. It is too frustrating and nothing is in the least bit attracted to the pink lure. I head back to camp, suddenly aware of the time. It is late now, and despite the fact that the wind and the tide are now with me, it takes a while to get back to the beach. The journey was not entirely wasted because there is always a sense of freedom when paddling alone in a beautiful place.

A quartering tailwind dogs me on my return. Often, when the wind blows from this particular angle, my kayak slides sideways to the waves. Correctional strokes only straighten the boat for a short period of time. This is one of those moments when it is a relief to be equipped with a rudder. My kayak is long and narrow so it usually tracks well, without the need for mechanical guidance. However, from time to time the rudder does come in handy and this is one of those moments. It is the end of a long day and I'm tired. All I want to do is get back to camp and the tailwind is thwarting my progress. I pull the string and my rudder unfolds from its position on deck, at the stern of the boat. Cables running through the boat link the rudder to my foot pedals, which now, with the rudder's release, glide back and forth as I push on them. The pedals move the rudder, thus guiding the boat. The method is simple: push with your right foot and the boat veers to the right; push with your left foot and it goes to the left.

As I paddle I notice that new neighbours have arrived on the beach, close to our

Evening light splashes over sand still damp from the receding tide. Even though this beach is shielded from the sunset by the forested slopes of Flores Island, it does not escape the world of evening colour.

camp. Sunlight flashes on glass and I realize that these neighbours are looking through binoculars. After several minutes, I realize that they are looking at me. I near the shore and notice that they are still looking at me, and I wonder what is so interesting about my boat. Eventually, I decide that the owner of the binoculars is obviously just curious, so I look directly towards the glinting lenses and wave cheerfully. The man drops the binoculars and scuttles up the beach. I am disappointed that he did not wave back.

While I have been gone, Jan has been hard at work, cooking supper. Luckily, she has decided on Mexican food, not a meal that depends on my success at fishing. A spicy aroma wafts down the beach as I empty out my kayak and move up to the relative privacy of our camp, which is hidden from our neighbours. After having guided so many trips, having someone else organize the meals is a new sensation. Despite my pleasure, I can't shake the feeling that I should have been doing something more helpful than attempting to catch a fish. But by the time I arrive there is nothing left to do, except to warm the tortilla shells over the fire before stuffing them so full that they threaten to burst at the seams.

Once again, we are eating after dark, which is vaguely satisfying because it suggests that we have truly made the most of the day. It is wonderful to be in such a beautiful place – a place where the animal prints are fresher and more plentiful than the human ones. What is more, the hours of sunshine we have experienced over the last few days are starting to add up, affecting us as if we are human solar panels. It is amazing how much energy it is possible to derive from the sun. This morning, when it was cloudy, all Jan and I wanted to do was to curl up in our sleeping bags, but as soon as the sky cleared we wanted to go as far and fast as possible. Now that the sun has slipped back into the ocean, we feel lethargic once again. I can identify with a bear's desire to hibernate when the daylight hours grow scarce. We feel the same desire, although perhaps to a lesser extent. We certainly feel virtuous to have used our bodies so fully throughout the course of the day. We need to save some of this energy, however, because tomorrow's journey to Sulphur Passage will be a long one; it will be a day to get up early and leave the beach at a respectable hour.

It is hard to think about getting up early – it is hard to think about moving at all. I seem to have formed an unbreakable bond with my foam camping chair. Only the thought of being cold and stiff later in the night galvanizes me into action, and once more we trek down the beach to hang up the food before flopping into our tents.

Chapter Five
GOING DEEPER

*From Whitesand Cove, via Ahousaht and
Shark Creek, to Sulphur Passage*

T'S SIX O'CLOCK IN THE MORNING AND THERE'S A MURDER OF crows outside that should be murdered themselves. I was right to have been suspicious of them yesterday, when they were feeding so quietly on the beach. Now they have spotted two empty plastic bags that were left out. There is nothing in the bags, but crows are persistent; they won't shut up unless I go and put the bags away. I stomp over to the tarp and open the bags. "See?" I show the crows. "Nothing in them. Now go away!"

It works. The crows lose interest in our camp and wander off. Or perhaps their main interest was to see if they could wake us up. I wouldn't put it past them. Sometimes crows just want to play tricks and they seem to take great pleasure in their mischief. They are slightly unnerving in their capacity as observers, always nearby, watching. Perhaps I am paranoid, but if I do something silly or uncoordinated, I'm sure I feel those shiny black eyes peer out from under a branch somewhere.

Maybe I should be more positive about the rude awakening. I ponder while

*The icy waters of Shark Creek tumbling to sea level. One story claims that female
basking sharks would swim all the way up the river to give birth below the waterfall —
no small feat given the shallowness of the river and the huge size of the sharks.*

crawling back into my cocoon, after all, it is going to be a beautiful day. The sky is clear, just waiting to be filled with colour. I stare dreamily out of the mesh door of the tent and before long I am snoozing again, but only for half an hour or so. There is a lengthy agenda today and it will benefit us to get underway early.

Things do not always go according to plan, however, and the challenge this morning lies in learning something that I already know: never buy polypropylene rope. A good system for a food cache requires two long pieces of rope. I was broke when I bought the polypropylene – unable to afford the nylon rope that I wanted. Cost and personal finances aside, I should have bought the nylon. I would have come away with two coils of rope that would take up less space in my boat and be far more manageable.

Until it becomes old and worn (and sometimes not even then) polypropylene rope is very slippery, sliding out of the best knots unless well weighted. It has no qualms about tying its own knots, though, and this morning the pile of rope at the foot of the bear cache is appallingly tangled. I can't believe the rat's nest that is there when I go to take the food down. I start trying to untangle it, knowing that it is better to do this in the daylight than to wait until it is dark and we are tired. I try to be patient, remembering advice given to me by my father about the patience needed

"The sky is clear, just waiting to be filled with colour." The quiet camp at early morning on Whitesand Cove – a quiet soon to be disturbed by a murder of crows.

when dealing with rope, following the path of the rope as it winds from loop to loop. But this rope is seriously tangled and the tangle is so involving that my original intent, which was to bring the food over to camp and start making breakfast, is forgotten. Eventually Jan comes over, wondering what has captivated me so thoroughly. Together we haul the duffel bag down the beach before returning to transfer the piles of rope away from the tree roots, where it can get tangled further, onto the beach. Being out in the open is more pleasant because the morning is spectacular and I was missing out on the shimmering pale blue colour that Adrian is enthusing about.

With help from the others I eventually get the rope put away and can concentrate on better things. The forecast for the day is good: a high pressure system is settling in. The wind is expected to blow 10 to 15 knots from the northwest, which shouldn't be a problem because we will have it behind us as we head north, up Millar Channel. By the time we finish breakfast a light breeze is shuffling across the satiny water. Regardless of where I am, or what the plans are, when the wind starts blowing this early in the day, it makes me anxious to get started. Today I have to be patient because it is not often that such perfect photo opportunities present themselves.

Our packing is getting quicker all the time, each person more familiar with the shape and weight of the various bags, knowing where they will fit best. A formula has established itself.

It is exciting to be moving on. Yesterday's walk was wonderful, but the wide blue yonder is calling again. And is it ever blue! This winter the sky and the sea were grey for so long that now I am having to reacquaint myself with the colour blue. This does not actually present any difficulties. We cruise into the blue with glee. This stretch of shoreline is almost entirely made up of white, sandy beaches, hence the name Whitesand Cove. We paddle in the shallow water close to land to avoid the ebbing tide that would hinder our progress. I am always interested in the interface between land and water. Here, animals have to reveal themselves as they cross from one environment and another. Paddling the shoreline often provides the most rewarding experiences with wildlife, as well as the security of being close to land. Also, here, it makes for a quicker route, even though it is much less direct. Going with the tide is always much easier, even it means seeking countercurrents.

Ever hopeful, I pull out my fishing rod and troll for a while. With the shallow water and the conspicuous lack of jumping coho, I am obviously being wildly optimistic. Trolling does not require much effort, however, since I can tuck the rod into my life jacket and continue paddling. What does require effort is the constant removal of seaweed from my lure and eventually I give up in exasperation.

We are nearing the village of Ahousaht, and even from this distance I can see a crowd of children playing on the beach. Because this was once the winter village of the O-tsus-aht, the site itself is actually called Maaqtusiis (or Marktosis), but is more commonly referred to as Ahousaht. Literally translated, *maaqtusiis* means "moving from one side to another," which perfectly describes the way the village spans this neck of land. The beautiful sandy beach we are coming to faces onto Millar Channel. To reach the safe waters of the harbour we would have to continue paddling until we got around the peninsula and into Matilda Inlet. It is possible to walk into the village from the beach and this is our intention today. It will save us a detour of several miles.

Until recently there was no secondary school and no grocery store in Ahousaht. When they ran out of food, residents had to boat down to Tofino or across the harbour, where the Ahousaht General Store is situated. This enterprise also acts as a marine gas station and stocks a wide variety of emergency goods. But a few years ago, the Marktosis Grocery opened its doors and is now able to supply most regular grocery items. I haven't spent much time in Ahousaht since the store opened so I am eager to see what it's like, although my main concern today is whether or not they carry junk food, our supply of which it is definitely necessary to replenish. The purist in me cringes at the idea of putting a wilderness adventure on pause while we stop at a grocery store for sugar. The realist in me pushes the boat up on the beach with little hesitation.

We are greeted by at least a dozen children between the ages of two and 10. They are excited by the arrival of these kayaks and eager to introduce themselves. Many of them have been in the water for most of the morning and seem unaffected by the cumulative effects of their cold immersion. Perhaps there is a special resilience to the cold that is particular to people from Ahousaht. On some of the snowiest days last winter, people from Ahousaht would casually saunter down Tofino streets wearing shorts. It made me shiver just thinking about it, and I'd have to huddle more deeply into the five layers of clothing I was probably wearing at the time. I'm inclined to chalk up their immunity to the cold to evolutionary superiority – or sheer stubbornness. Actually, it may be that the weather on the coast used to be colder than anything experienced here recently. One man who had attended residential school in Ahousaht 60 years ago remembers ice-skating across Matilda Inlet to get to school. In the few years I have lived in the sound it has seldom become so cold that the salt-water inlets have frozen up.

There is no longer a residential school in Ahousaht; in fact, just recently the band built their own secondary school here. This exciting development has created great opportunities for people of all ages who wish to further their schooling. Before, it had been difficult for students to deal with high school. They had to board with families in Port Alberni or Nanaimo, or travel daily by boat to Tofino and then by bus to Ucluelet. Now, the same people have only to walk down the street to get to school and the number of high-school graduates has flourished dramatically here. The school is locally directed, although the teachers come from all over. This approach is a breath of fresh air; the long tyranny of residential schools had engendered a general resentment towards institutions.

In 1874 a Catholic missionary by the name of Father Brabant travelled up the coast to begin converting Natives to Christianity. He established himself at Hesquiaht, an area just north of Hotsprings Cove, where he worked to remove what the Church saw as paganism, for a period of 33 years. He also established missions

No matter that this kayak is hauled up on the sand out of the water; just sitting in it is exciting enough for this young adventurer.

up and down the coast and was the impetus for creation of the Christie Residential school in 1899. This school was built at Kakawis on Meares Island, close to the village of Opitsaht, and was the first residential school in Clayoquot Sound. Not long afterwards a Protestant residential school was built in Ahousaht.

The intent of these schools was to "Christianize the savages" and Clayoquot Sound was by no means the only place where such an institution existed; from the late 1800s to the 1960s, residential schools dominated Native communities across Canada. The federal government was happy for the education of Natives to be taken up by the Protestant and Catholic churches. Federal Indian agents forced the enrollment of all children, denying food rations to families who did not comply. By the 1920s, enrollment had become law; by the 1930s, parents could be jailed if their children did not attend the schools. While the intent of the missionaries might have been to save souls (measuring their success by the number of conversions they notched into their belts), the government had a different motivation – eradicating what they saw as The Indian Problem in Canada. Even though Native populations had been drastically reduced and weakened by epidemics, non-Native people feared the power of Native cultures, and one of the easiest ways to destroy tradition and culture is to

Summer of fun: the children of Ahousaht in their element, completely unaffected by the frigid temperature of the water, blissfully whiling away the extended daylight hours of July.

isolate the younger generations from their heritage – specifically, their language. Without language, the nuances of culture are easily broken down. And this was the focus of the residential schools: students were forbidden to speak their own language. Punishments were brutally severe and have had a lingering effect on those who survived the system.

In his book of reminiscences, *As Far As I Know*, Ahousaht elder Peter Webster recalls his time at the residential school in Ahousaht.

> My memories of attending the school are not pleasant ones. I entered knowing no English. I found that every time I used my Native tongue I was punished.
>
> While we attended school we had to listen, morning and night, to readings from the Bible. We did not understand any of it. Even today I cannot pronounce many of the words although I know that we should pay attention to it.

Many of the punishments Native students suffered were more sinister than Peter's experience of being sent to bed without supper. A number of recent legal suits have resulted in the jailing of residential school workers for indecent sexual offences against Nuu-chah-nulth pupils. Abhorrent behaviour flourished easily in the rigid environment of control, hierarchy and punishment.

For an outsider it is easy to presume that, since they have been abolished, the problems associated with residential schools are gone now. Two problems, at least, still linger. One is that several generations of children were removed from their parents and raised in alien environments from the time they were six years old until they were 16. Brothers and sisters were separated by sex and forbidden to talk to one another. Consequently, not only were sibling bonds destroyed, but children did not know what it was like to be raised by parents. Their only experience of growing up was one of loveless institutions and constant punishment. This experience caused more problems – not only when these individuals came live their own lives outside of the rigid system of rules and orders – but when they came to have their own children.

Speaking at a potlatch in Bella Bella, a woman who had attended residential school described how lost she felt when her daughter reached puberty. She asked her mother for advice on how address the transition, but her mother didn't know; her own children had gone through their teens at residential school and she had not had to deal with it. When consulted, this woman's grandmother also did not know, for the same reason. The residential schools left behind a legacy of humans who were – for all intents and purposes – orphans.

The other problem is that few pupils ever went beyond grade six; in fact, the government actually discouraged them from doing so. Those who left the schools were unfamiliar with their own cultures and insufficiently versed in the new culture. Feelings of inadequacy ran rampant, in some cases made more acute by the degrading abuse and the racist sentiments that had been suffered within the schools.

Instead of removing The Indian Problem by means of the residential school system, the government actually created a new problem: a group of people who were insufficiently trained to function in either society, who were prone to feelings of inadequacy and depression, and who had tendencies towards alcoholism and suicide.

In an interesting turn of events, after the Catholic residential school at Kakawis closed (it later accidentally burned down), it was replaced by a family development centre, which provides six-week treatment sessions for families ravaged by alcoholism. Some of those who attend Kakawis now are healing themselves at a site that was the source of their troubles.

When I think of the immeasurable sadness and upheaval that the Ahousaht society has had to endure, I am truly amazed at the beaming smiles on the faces of these children. The smiles are a testament to the Nuu-chah-nulth tradition of protecting the future generations.

The cheerful welcoming party wastes no time ensconcing themselves in our boats, paddling through imaginary waters while the kayaks sit high and dry on the sand. Adrian stays behind to photograph the fun while Jan and I wander up to the village. We walk along the dirt roads, clouds of dust from the occasional pickup truck temporarily obscuring the view. The dogs in Ahousaht have a habit of waiting for the exact moment that a vehicle approaches before they casually cross from one side of the road to another, pausing nonchalantly to scratch while the drivers try to shoo them out of the way. The sun is scorchingly hot – a pleasant novelty.

Walking to the Marktosis Grocery takes about 10 minutes, although there is a more direct route that we could have taken. The store is in a large building that also serves other purposes. Amongst the eclectic variety of goods, we eventually manage to find an assortment of dried fruit and some well-priced chocolate. The store's proprietor, Luke Swan, is friendly and helpful, obviously well suited to this new venture. He must find it amusing that we have come all the way here just to buy snacks. He wishes us well on our journey and we head back to the boats, stashing shiny packages away, under the wistful gazes of our onlookers. They help us launch, with great enthusiasm, draping themselves over our bows and propelling us out into deeper water. The arrangement eventually becomes a little precarious – the further out we go, the further onto our decks the stowaways are inclined to crawl, and the more wobbly we become. The situation does not reach crisis point, however, and we paddle away to a cheery chorus of good-byes. Our only follower is a white dog who refuses to stop swimming behind us. After repeated attempts to make her turn around, Adrian paddles back to the beach, until she decides to get out of the water and let us leave unaccompanied.

We continue in the same direction, still following the eastern shoreline of Flores Island, still keeping close to the land and out of the tide. The rocks are rich with intertidal life; sea stars and sea anemones mix in with the bladderwrack that is prevalent between the high- and low-water marks. The water in Millar Channel is a dark ruffled blue and the colours of the forest have flattened into the greyish green that they sometimes adopt in the middle of a hot day. Red cedars lean over me as I paddle, their fronds hanging down decoratively, their branches occasionally adorned with heavy clumps of ochre-coloured moss. Across the channel I admire the unique shape of McKay Island. I can't shake my impression of this island as a soft blob of land, dropped from on high, its flat edges melting symmetrically away from the lump in its centre.

Reaching our lunch spot involves paddling up a creek that flows out over a wide bouldery beach. This is not the kind of surface over which it would be pleasant to carry kayaks, so we tie our bowlines to large rocks and anchor the boats in the deepest section of the creek while we are still some distance from the forest. The tide is close to slack, so we shouldn't have to worry too much about them unless the wind builds, in which case they could end up banging against the rocks.

Armed with the precious lunch cargo, including some of our more recent acquisitions, we walk along the river to a lovely meadow, beautifully lit by the sun. The spreading branches of a large spruce provide a shady retreat under which we lay out the meal. Below us the water slips by, reflecting the green of the forest, providing a focal point for our eyes while our mouths are occupied with elaborate picnic combinations. Sprawled among clover and roses, we wonder how paradise compares to our present location.

Once we persuade ourselves to move, all that remains is for lunch to be cleaned up and the water bags to be filled. It seems safer to drink the water of Flores rather than that of the mainland, perhaps because there are more animals on the mainland, which increases the potential for contamination. This is a personal theory, based entirely on instinct, reflecting my totally unscientific approach to the issue. In general I don't bother treating the creek water in the Clayoquot Sound area, unless I am guiding a trip. While I have never suffered from drinking untreated water, other people have not been so fortunate. It is probably better to err on the side of caution, but I am too fond of creek water to ruin the taste by adding iodine and too lazy to spend time boiling it. I take the bags and follow the creekside trail, wondering which animals also use this route. The path is well worn. In fall, bears must spend a lot of time here catching chum. I walk up the creek, far enough away from the areas where tidal influence might cause the water to be brackish. Up here the water is so cold that my feet can't stay still for long. I fill the bags as quickly as I can and slip-slide over the mossy rocks back to the trail.

Water bags are a wonderful invention. Like the bags found inside boxes of wine, they are sturdy and have an easy spout system. More importantly, they collapse when empty, so they don't take up precious space when not in use. The type we use are protected by a nylon cover and have a handle that is useful for carrying or for hanging the bags from when in camp.

As we pick our way back to the boats, Adrian spots the print of a wolf, neatly pressed into a soft patch of gravel. Wolves are capable of covering fair distances and we are probably not more than three nautical miles from Whitesand Cove, as the crow flies. Could this also be the territory of our friend with the lazy foot? It seems likely.

The boats are still floating, which is a bonus. The less carrying we have to do, the better. We make space for the newly filled water bags and head on up the coast of Flores. We could cross over to the mainland now, but the further we paddle up the channel, the less the breeze will affect us. Now that the tide is ebbing, it is going in the opposite direction from the wind and will create a slight chop that will be more noticeable in midchannel. Conditions on this side will be calmer and more scenic.

There is a scattering of small islands along the eastern edge of Flores that I'm already excited about paddling through; we will be able to slip away from the main body of water and be cloistered by their proximity.

Some of these islands are rocky, with sparse, dry environments. Fantastically gnarled trees squirm out of crevices and manage to reach surprising heights. There are even some Douglas fir among them – truly West Coast-style Douglas fir, nothing like the towering beauties in Cathedral Grove, near Port Alberni. These trees have not been spoiled by the climate; they have had to struggle for every inch, a fact that is conspicuous to even the most untrained eye.

A few hundred feet away, the trees on Flores are lush and uniform by comparison. In one place, an overwhelming coolness assails our senses; we can smell the fresh water that must be somewhere nearby. We are in a narrow passageway, with the shores of Flores and a smaller, nearby island only a stone's throw apart. We are completely out of the wind. It is amazing, the extent to which we had become accustomed to the noise of the wind. The sudden silence is profound. Even the small splashes from our paddles seem invasive now and each of us gradually pauses, drifting quietly in appreciation of the moment.

It is so easy to allocate hours and minutes and miles to each day, creating timetables that don't allow for moments like this. Often, I have been too anxious to reach a destination and have not wanted to take a detour that could have been rewarding. One solution is to take longer trips, trips that lay themselves open to detours and changes of plan. With some exceptions, I find mileage gradually losing its importance as a tool with which to measure success.

We emerge from our silent detour into the main body of the channel. Ahead of us is a sailboat, wafting along in a wind that diminishes rapidly the further north we travel. Suddenly, a water taxi races by, on its way to the hot springs. The whining outboard shatters the peaceful mood; worse, the passage of the boat places us back in a context, fixes us between two points on a map, interferes with the notion that we are in our own private world, some sort of fantasy land.

When it comes time to cross Millar Channel the conditions do not present any sort of a challenge. It is easy to fix a landmark; the atrocious clearcuts on the hills above the Atleo River are visible from far away. The big S-shaped scar of the road at the top is the most conspicuous mark, and then there is the sweep of tree stumps, down the mountainside to the water, where a few alders and some remnant cedars poke up amid a rubble of dead trees, as if to apologize for the emptiness behind them.

The Atleo was once a prize. It was for rivers like this that territorial wars were fought. The bounty of salmon returning to this river had immeasurable value. I wonder how many years of clearcutting it took to destroy the precious spawning habitat so completely. Four? Five? The destruction fills our view for the duration of the crossing. It is a rude awakening. We have been so lulled by views of intact forests that the harsh reality of clearcuts is a slap in the face. But the past and the future of Clayoquot Sound are threaded with the issue of forestry. The topic will probably be a bone of contention for years to come. The fact that nearly 900 people chose to be arrested in 1993 in protest of logging has not altered much. Logging was put on hold for a while; some areas have been made into parks; various boards discuss the plans for Interfor's next clearcuts; scientific panel recommendations are supposed to be followed. But the fragmentation of Clayoquot Sound as an entirety has not been addressed and the logging itself is not necessarily carried out at a community level, in a locally sustainable manner.

With one possible exception.

As part of the recent treaty process between the provincial government and the Nuu-chah-nulth, a joint-venture company was set up between MacMillan Bloedel and five central-region Native tribes, including the Tla-o-qui-aht, the Ahousaht and the Hesquiaht. The formation of the company was said to have been a deal-breaker in negotiations: the government wanted proof that if the Natives reassumed control of their land the forests would still be used in a way that would benefit the province, in a way that would ensure the continued flow of fibre. The company was named Iisaak ("respect"), and ownership is 51 percent First Nations, 49 percent MacMillan Bloedel. The intent behind the venture was for Natives to participate in logging operations on lands within MacMillan Bloedel's tenure. But logging did not start right away; Clayoquot Sound was still too much of a hotbed, and MacMillan Bloedel gradually pulled out of the area rather than face the continual blockades and international boycotts so effectively created by the environmentalists.

However, with Iisaak, MacMillan Bloedel had the means to consider approaching forestry anew, in a way that might polish their tarnished reputation. Discussions were held between Iisaak and several environmental groups in an attempt to reach some sort of truce. The resulting Memorandum of Understanding was signed, to much fanfare, on June 16, 1999.

The thrust of the agreement was that currently pristine areas within MacMillan Bloedel's tenure would remain untouched and Iisaak would seek eco-certification – an official stamp recognizing that environmental standards have been met – for its logging processes and its lumber. In exchange for these gestures the environmental groups would work to promote, rather than block, Iisaak products. They would also have to turn a blind eye to the fact that some of the lumber extracted initially would be from old-growth areas. Consolidating the tenures in Clayoquot was another point of discussion, meaning that MacMillan Bloedel would try to buy out its rival, Interfor, leaving a single forestry tenure in Clayoquot that would be eventually transferred to Iisaak. If all these good intentions came to fruition, there would finally be a forest company in Clayoquot Sound that was 100 percent locally owned and operated – and it would be operated according to stringent eco-forestry principles.

That four major environmental groups signed the understanding seemed too good to be true. Absent from the celebration were the Friends of Clayoquot Sound, the group behind most of the protests in the sound to date. But while they abstained from signing the agreement, they didn't actively oppose it.

Then, four days after the signing, MacMillan Bloedel announced its takeover by the American logging giant, Weyerhaeuser, who didn't immediately agree to uphold the memorandum. Weyerhaeuser is hardly a local company with local responsibilities. Some of its Canadian lumber is shipped to the United States for manufacturing. Responses to the takeover among many factions included shock, fear and embarrassment. Some time later, Weyerhaeuser tentatively committed to upholding the memorandum, but it is still unclear exactly what the future holds for Iisaak. To date, the company is going ahead with its plans to have fibre flowing by year end. The process of eco-certification seems to have become less important since the signing. The future of the trees and the forest in Clayoquot Sound is still as uncertain as ever.

Humans have a habit of repeating their mistakes. Looking at the devastated Atleo River valley, I hope, with doubt, that these clearcutting practices are never repeated. We paddle past the mouth of the river, keeping our eyes peeled for the black bears that are plentiful in this area. It is probably too hot for them, though, and instead we stare at the desolate estuary, wondering what it might have looked like before it was pockmarked with the stumps of trees and made bereft of their living trunks, branches and needles.

Now that we are so close to land, the logged area is less visible and soon it is behind the kayaks. The sight still lingers in our minds, but it is not long before we near the islet that denotes the entrance to Shark Creek and find ourselves in an entirely different environment. Few places are as breathtaking. As I paddle up the river, away from the salt water, I feel the thrill this place always spurs in me; it has something to do with the power of the waterfall as it cascades over the rocks, pounding the walls of the canyon as it rushes onwards.

Steep bluffs guard the entrance to the grotto, a graceful drift log arched between them. On the other side of this gateway, the mossy rock walls encircle a small pool that is about 40 feet wide. We tie the boats to tree branches near the entrance, whip off our clothes and psych ourselves up for what will doubtlessly be the coldest swim of the trip. Even though the fresh water mingles with the salt water here, I know from past experience that the sea exerts no tangible warming influence. The river water sets the temperature and it is one of the most frigid pools around. Perversely, like salmon going upstream to their deaths, we feel as though, having come this far, we *have* to swim here, as if our experience will not be complete without this icy baptism.

True to our expectations, the water is shockingly cold. It's colder than it was when I was here last year, but we go under the waterfall anyway, allowing ourselves to be dunked by the pressure, soaked and chilled and swept back down to the rocks where our boats are tied. We waste no time in floating the boats to a spot lower down the riverbank, where we dry off and sit in the sun, eating Marktosis Grocery cookies in an attempt to warm ourselves up. It is hard to believe how fortunate we have been. There is not a cloud in sight and the sky is clear and soft. The hills of Flores Island fold gently away into the distance, catching shadows from the sun as it goes towards the west. The inimitable blue tones that I associate so strongly with the West Coast start to manifest themselves in the evening light. Close up, the glossy water is a deep green-gold, reflecting the canopy of trees that tower above us.

When we are warm enough, the magnetic appeal of the forest draws us in. Adrian finds some tremendous Douglas firs, broad and tall, with deeply furrowed, braided bark. One of them even has the pattern of a leaf imprinted on the bark. Another large

*Sheathed with mosses and ferns, steep bluffs accompany the water on its downward plunge
into the grotto at Shark Creek. The rocky walls intensify the roar of the cascade, while
the smooth rocks testify to the erosive force of the water.*

tree, a cedar, has been cut down some time ago and abandoned, perhaps because of the punky fibres on one end. I melt into its subtle shape to contemplate my surroundings, hoping to be saturated by the soulful loveliness of this place if I remain motionless long enough.

Wandering through the trees a while later, I come across a spot where the forest opens up like a garden, stretching away in a profusion of deer ferns, tree branches hazy with the soft sunlit glow of old man's beard, translucent in the low-slanting shafts of light. The cold-water baptism is being rivalled by a deep-forest equivalent. The hairs on my arms and neck prickle with the intensity of the moment. It is a while before we drag ourselves away.

Shark Creek is so named because of the basking sharks that frequent the waters in the area. One story from long ago even holds that the sharks actually come into the grotto to give birth to their young. I ponder this as we launch the boats again, trying to imagine 30 feet and four tonnes of pregnant shark weaving her way up the creek and squeezing through the entranceway to the pool. I suppose that if they were to arrive at high tide, they would find it a safe, cavelike place to give birth. I wonder who saw them giving birth here, how the story started.

Despite their size, basking sharks are not aggressive animals, nor do they have rows of fearsome teeth. They are equipped instead with massive mouths and rows of gills that filter planktonic food from the water column. Once they were numerous on the coast, a common part of Nuu-chah-nulth traditional knowledge. Now few remain. Basking sharks sighted in these waters in 1992 and 1993 may be the only known remaining aggregation of these animals on Vancouver Island. In the 1950s the Department of Fisheries decided to put an end to the problems that the presence of basking sharks near the seine nets of salmon fishermen were said to have created. A brutal program of extermination was initiated in Barkley Sound. Boats were equipped with knife blades of boiler-plate steel. These protruded in an arc, five feet out from the bow; the intent was to slice through any sharks that were encountered. A report by Jim Hazlewood in the *Vancouver Sun* (May 16, 1956) describes the carnage:

> The great shark slaughter began at noon and continued for hours. We littered the beaches with their livers and the bottom with their carcasses . . . By dusk we had a record one-day kill of 34 definite, about five possibles and ten misses.

I stood on the bow, directly above the knife. A torpedo-shaped, olive-green form made a frantic twist in the water but it was too late. A cloud of blood burst over the bow as the ship shuddered at the impact. A tail that was six feet across thrashed the water until it was severed from the shark's body. Then the two pieces toppled off the knife and sank . . . We all felt better after that. We were worried that we might not see any sharks at all.

The language of the day paints the sharks as pests and brutes: the more killed, the better. It's a scene that's hard to picture, especially since few people these days have ever seen a basking shark. For a while, the Clayoquot Biosphere Project, a local research body, carried out studies on the basking sharks, under the direction of Dr. Jim Darling. From their camps in Sydney and Shelter Inlets the researchers managed to photo-identify a surprising total of 27 different sharks. The basking sharks' fins are often heavily scarred as a result of their penchant for basking in the sun, close to the surface of the water, where they may be unseen – but not unfelt – by motor boats. These distinctive fins made the identification of the sharks a feasible project. Since the study took place, in 1992 and 1993, the number of basking sharks may have

*Every duck has his day. This common merganser (*Mergus merganser*) shows off the sharp colours of his breeding plumage. All too soon these feathers will become brown and inconspicuous.*

declined drastically, which is unfortunate. There have been few – if any – sightings, which raises a host of questions about water temperature and water quality. Basking sharks are often sighted in early morning or late evening, in sunny, calm weather. It's sunny and calm around us here, now, but the scene is sadly unadorned by shark fins. It is worth keeping an eye out for them, though; they have been known to leap completely clear of the water, for reasons that are not entirely understood.

Perhaps because we are deep in the channel, the sun fades more quickly than it did on previous days. A couple of miles linger between us and the campsite we hope to reach in Sulphur Passage. We are caught between the necessity of reaching camp before dark and the urge to fully experience our idyllic surroundings. Regardless of the speed at which we travel, the process of moving through this richly painted water can be nothing but pleasurable, even at the end of a long day. We could have camped further back down Millar Channel, but that would make our paddling day too long tomorrow. If we were planning to go through Hayden Passage en route to the hot springs, it wouldn't matter, but we have opted to go the long way – through Sulphur Passage and around Obstruction Island – so a head start will be helpful.

We reach Sulphur Passage as the last ray of sun dips below the mountains. The light breeze is enough to make us keep moving, to hurry our unpacking. It's not really cold, but after such a long day, such a chilly swim and with hair still damp, we are easily susceptible. I pull on my thick wool toque – the ultimate in luxurious headgear. Often this toque is all that is needed to tip the scales between shivering and comfort. It is usually close at hand, even in the summer. If a client on a trip unexpectedly upsets a kayak, this hat is the quickest way to start rewarming them once they are back in their boat, even before they have been taken to shore for a change of clothes.

The smell of basmati rice drifts tantalizingly on the wind. We have been truly efficient with our organization and have even soaked the mung beans ahead of time, so that now they are quickly ready, just one of the ingredients in a thick rich curry that draws us back for seconds. And thirds. And. . . .

Despite the wind (or perhaps because of it), there is a dryness in the air here and we decide to risk sleeping out in the open, under the stars. Sometimes, when the mountains rise up darkly on all sides like this, the sky is so incredibly dark; the stars so incredibly bright. Such is the case tonight. I pull a tarp over my sleeping bag in anticipation of the dew and lie down in the grass. My eyelids droop, but I force them open for as long as possible to drink in the sparkling ceiling up above. The wind whispers quietly, lulling us deeply to sleep. The only interruption of the night is the rising of the last-quarter moon, almost orange, dangling above the moving waters of the passage.

Chapter Six

INTO THE WIND

*From Sulphur Passage, via Steamer Cove,
to Crazy Eagle Beach, Flores Island*

AST NIGHT'S WELCOME INTERRUPTION — THE RISING
moon — is followed by an equally welcome interruption this
morning. It is the sun coming up, warming my face, softening the process of awakening. I blink into the brightness and watch as it hits the
water, refracting like a crystal in a window.

The squeak of Adrian's tripod adds sound to the otherwise silent scene. He is up
and about already, delighted with this good weather. Not only that, we are in a place
that evokes much for him. In 1988 he was returning from a camping trip with a
friend when a blast of dynamite went off in this area. Shocked, he realized that a logging road was being built, heading to Sulphur Passage and points beyond. A nascent
awareness of logging had been evolving in Tofino since the fight for Meares Island,
and at Adrian's news an emergency meeting was called. It was decided that something should be done to prevent the logging companies from accessing pristine areas
such as the Megin River.

*Sulphur Passage proves difficult to paddle away from. One look at the stunning scenery
and it becomes clear why a battle for environmental protection was fought near here.*

Those who opposed the road were fired by strong personal emotions, not just preordained environmental doctrines. The war against logging was just beginning to unfold, and the protest that followed at Sulphur Passage was radical and truly grassroots – the collective adventures of many individuals. The protest was a pivotal moment in the recent history of Clayoquot Sound.

The protest started with a boat blockade, but quickly became more involved. Soon there were people in the forest and Canada's first tree-sitters took their positions, hanging in baskets from cliffs or in hammocks slung between trees, putting themselves anywhere they could to stop the blasting. Fletcher Challenge, the New Zealand company behind the road building, sought injunctions against the protestors that would make it illegal for them to be present at the blast site. The injunctions had little effect. Both sides dug in. Things became crazy, with RCMP officers chasing protestors around in the woods, trying to arrest them, trying to get them out of the blasting zone. The anarchy was not confined to one side. In an unprecedented, aggressive move, the loggers cut down one of the trees onto which a protestor's hammock was tied.

The environmentalists tried to acquire an injunction against the road and requested a six-month moratorium on logging, during which the future of the sound would be discussed. Their efforts failed.

Another attempt to halt the road came from a different quarter: Earl Maquinna George, hereditary chief of the Ahousaht, came to the disputed site to take a stance against the destruction of trees that were on his traditional lands – lands that remained to be relinquished by treaty. A second injunction was sought on these grounds. It was also denied.

The road building was never stopped by the courts. It was the negative publicity heaped on Fletcher Challenge that precipitated the resulting truce. By the end of July 1988, 35 people had been arrested over an issue that had become a regular fireship. Some were jailed for their antics, including several women who languished for one week in the maximum security of Oakalla jail. Adrian himself was arrested, although he didn't go to jail. His face lights up as he recalls the events of that summer, one of the most powerful moments of which took place when he was camped right here in Sulphur Passage. That night, wolves joined in the protest, howling through the midnight hours. Early the next morning, at the door of the tent, Adrian's dog Sparky came nose to nose with one of the wolves.

*Morning light suffuses this moss-covered rock at Obstruction Island. One minute our surroundings
are lush and green, the next minute there are headlands or islands that are exposed
and bare — an entirely different world.*

115

There is something deeply evocative bound up in the howling of wolves. When heard in the wild, the serenade is impossible to forget. Sulphur Passage would lend itself well to wolf songs. Mountains slide down to a saltwater passageway that snakes past their feet in myriad twists and turns. The howls would echo from one slope to the next, back and forth across the narrow channel, on and out into Shelter Inlet and beyond.

I wonder about Shelter Inlet as I listen to the forecast for the day. Wind seems to affect Sulphur Passage differently than other areas; the absolute mirror glaze of the water may not be an accurate reflection of the conditions that will be encountered once we exit the passage. It is still early, but today is to be the longest paddling day of the trip and I want to be sure that we are well paced. A small trough of low pressure is predicted to pass through tonight, so this may be the last of the nice weather. The wind will be from the northwest again, a moderate 15 knots, which would not usually concern me; however, because we are in the inlets, the wind might have a tendency to funnel, picking up

Like plump inch worms, these harbour seals rely on stomach muscles to pull themselves onto the rocks to bask in the sun. They are wary, though, constantly craning their heads to assess moving objects for their danger potential.

additional strength as it does so. The longer the inlet, the greater the distance over which the wind can build. It will benefit us to get going early today and factor in rest stops along the way. There is nothing like a constant headwind over a long distance to sap energy and I wonder whether it is frivolous to be paddling around Obstruction Island when we could dispense with some of those miles by going the quick way. When Millar Channel reaches Obstruction Island, it forks, like a Y, into Hayden and Sulphur Passages; both are spectacular, but while Hayden Passage provides a more direct route to the hot springs, Sulphur Passage is the more beautiful of the two. I gaze around me at Sulphur Passage, knowing that there really is no contest. Why come this far and not go the whole way?

In this place, on this day, the needs of the photographers in the group obviously cannot be denied. I know that I will appreciate my surroundings more completely if I relax, but the itch to leave is in my fingers and anxiety stabs me like a toothache. I try to calm myself as the others exclaim over their viewfinders. Hating to wreck the mood, I paddle on ahead, trying to encourage followers.

At the same time it is impossible to avoid being affected by the phenomenal stillness. It is an absolute stillness that seems to remove all clutter and replace it with something else. The feeling that is locked between these mountains is uniquely separate – solemn, independent and strong. Rock faces tower up beside me, scarred grey, with an abundance of pale green lichen. A string of islets stretches like a necklace across the exit to the passage. Overhead, an eagle wings onwards until reaching the islands, where it suddenly swoops low to the water, rising in victory with a fish. As we come through the very last islands on the northwest side of the passage, a narrow channel falls – the width of my outstretched arms – between an island and a little rock. It is deep, with wavy fronds of kelp and rock walls studded with sea stars. The tide runs like a river in this one place, which makes for an enjoyable ride as it pushes the kayak on and through.

There has been a harbour seal following us for a while. At one point it came up right off my bow, its sleek dark head shining in the direct sunlight. Harbour seals are fairly common in the sound; in fact, they may be more numerous than in the past, because they are hunted less often than before by Natives. Their hallmark curiosity lures them to kayakers and I can't help but wonder what they do with all the data they appear to be collecting when they observe us. It's easy to envision them with clipboards in their flippers, counting boats and humans, estimating our travelling speed, differentiating us by colour. Their preference is to come up behind the boats, to watch undisturbed.

Few sights are so endearing as these inquisitive faces. At four to five feet long, the seals are not as large as their sea lion cousins, nor as aggressive. They can be a variety of colours, from dark to pale, with any array of spots dappling their soft fur. And whereas the front flippers of sea lions are jointed and can be used on land as limbs, the flippers of harbour seals are like little paddles, no help when the seals are out of the water; instead, to haul themselves out on the rocks and snooze, the seals rely on stomach-muscle contractions, and it is almost painful to watch them jerk their plump bodies over the sharp rocks and barnacles. Out of the water they are wary, constantly moving their heads – checking to see if any hungry orcas are in the neighbourhood. If, by chance, there are, the seals waste little time, hurling themselves back into the water to deal with the predators in their own element.

We emerge from Sulphur Passage infused with the sublime beauty, completely unprepared for the reality that greets us around the corner: at the northernmost point of the passage, a fish farm sprawls across the bay, blaring radiophone messages over a loudspeaker. The metallic noise rings across the flat water, assailing our delicate ears. We feel as if we are passing a concentration camp. We are. In this case the internees are salmon; their jail is below the waterline.

If any issue is waiting in the wings, after logging, to dominate the environmental scene, it is fish-farming. The argument is a traditional one: jobs versus the integrity of the environment. As well as experiencing criticism from green factions, fish farms have received public opposition from the Nuu-chah-nulth. Their submission to the provincial government's 1997 Salmon Aquaculture Review Board was strongly worded:

> Nuu-chah-nulth opposition is founded in direct observation of salmon net cage culture on the sea resources in Nuu-chah-nulth waters. Clam beaches are fouled; juvenile herring are consumed; adult herring are blocked from spawning; wild salmon rearing areas are contaminated; seals, sea lions, otters and birds are needlessly killed . . . and escaped, cage-reared Atlantic, chinook and coho salmon enter the spawning streams to further threaten dwindling wild stocks. The health of the food

chain is threatened to such a point that many . . . elders now fear to eat seafoods that they have consumed all their lives.

This opposition is also apparent at a more local level. In July 1998 one fish farm was presented with an eviction notice by the Ahousaht. The farm's licence had expired and the farm itself was considered by the Natives to impact the environment of a traditional seafood gathering area, as well as to exist on traditional lands without their permission. The notice to evacuate was delivered in style by a flotilla of boats, including two large dugout canoes. Resentment was also expressed by the Ahousaht at the industry's attempt to broker a deal in the form of a joint venture. Acceptance of the deal would allow the fish farms to expand into many areas, triumphant in their cultural endorsement. In this instance, the lure of money and jobs was insufficient; the eradication of natural fish stocks was too much of a concern for the Ahousaht.

Apart from the obvious issue of pollution – pollution from salmon waste, pollution from salmon food, pollution from antibiotics in the food, pollution from the transfer of disease – there is another, related issue that has received a lot of attention recently. In 1998 juvenile Atlantic salmon were found in the Tsitika River on the east side of Vancouver Island. This river had no salmon hatchery and the fish were thought to be the progeny of escaped farm fish, an accusation that was strenuously denied by the industry. The discovery created an uproar. It highlighted the question of what would happen if wild salmon rivers were colonized by farmed salmon.

On the other side of Shelter Inlet, within easy view of this fish farm, lies the Megin River valley, an environment so rich that protection has been granted to the entire watershed, including an ecological reserve at the mouth of the river. The Megin is one of the few rivers to which all five species of wild salmon are said to return. For five species to return to one place an intricate balance must exist; the different runs cannot adversely affect one another and each species must manage to reach their preferred spawning area in time. What would happen if a new, non-wild species started breeding here?

Disease is an obvious worry. Farmed fish are selectively bred for their disease resistance, but they still have the potential to carry disease with them. Atlantic salmon may also carry unknown or non-native diseases that could have as devastating an effect on the wild salmon as the epidemics did on Native peoples.

Crossbreeding is another fear, although the greater concern may be around precocious male parr spawning over the eggs of wild salmon such as coho. This could mean unsuccessful reproduction in a species whose numbers are already dwindling.

The dwindling numbers of wild fish and the increasing numbers of farm fish might now combine to lay wild rivers open to colonization. In the 1930s, young Atlantic salmon and brown trout were introduced into the Cowichan River on the east side of Vancouver Island. The trout thrived while the salmon did not. The fish-farm industry upholds the failure of this experiment as proof that Atlantic salmon will be unable to populate wild rivers. Strong competition may have faced the tiny fry, however; the Cowichan River in the 1930s would have been bursting with full-size, wild Pacific salmon. Trout have different needs and would have found their own niche.

Times are different now. Rivers are empty, compared to what they were like in the thirties, and instead of being introduced as fry, Atlantics now enter as fully grown fish, fat from all the pellets, stronger and more able to compete.

I wonder whether it was a farm fish that the eagle swooped down on moments ago. The company operating this farm has a total of five farms in Clayoquot Sound. They admit to an escape rate of 2,000 salmon a year. If 400 fish per farm is an average, the three companies in Clayoquot Sound, operating a total of 18 farms, might collectively report 7,200 escapes annually. I look back at the mouth of the Megin River, at the hills falling steeply to the bright green low-lying land at their base. Large rocks mark the exit of the river like gates. Looking more closely, I can make out individual trees. That's how close the Megin is, how close these farm fish are to Nirvana.

The growth of aquaculture endows the salmon with a sense of global importance, one which is difficult to fully appreciate because they are so quickly processed and sent away. The historic importance of wild salmon is easier to grasp. Without salmon there would have been hard times and starvation for Native people. The return of these fish was closely monitored and prayed for; few of their habits remained unknown. Different techniques were used for catching different species. When the herring returned in March, the first spring salmon would be caught by trolling live herring behind canoes. In this area of the sound, an early run of small sockeye at the Megin in April would herald the start of the returns. The catching, eating and preserving of the different species of salmon occupied much of the activity for the year. The culmination was in the return of the dog salmon (chum) late in the year. These fish were crucial to the winter survival of the people. Since the chum returned so late, their fat content was much diminished, which made them ideal for smoke-drying, less likely to be ruined by their fat becoming rancid.

Chum often return to the smallest bodies of fresh water, little creeks that thread through the rainforest, becoming just swollen enough in the October rains to allow the fish to move upstream. These little streams are silent victims of clearcutting. Many of them are so small that they are discounted as being able to bear salmon, but chum return to them, just as they return to the larger rivers. The Megin River is one of them; Watta Creek, which lies north of us, was once well known for its late run of chum. Such creeks were strictly guarded by the tribes against unauthorized use.

Traps, weirs, nets, harpoons and gaff hooks were all tools that were employed in some way as the salmon ascended the spawning streams. From catching to preserving to eating, every part of the process was truly hands on. The human lives were inextricably bound up with those of the salmon. Depletion of wild salmon stocks through logging and overfishing is just one more 20th-century indignity that Natives are struggling to cope with. My dismay at having been unable to catch a coho pales in comparison to such enormous loss.

At this moment, however, fishing is not a consideration. We are close to the northern corner of Obstruction Island and the water just around the point is already dark with wind. Our leisurely journey is about to take on a new twist.

Like a conversation-stopper at a party, wind affects the mood of a group. The transition is swift. From casually lily-dipping through satin water we suddenly switch to forceful strokes. Idle chatter dies away; the noise of the wind fills our ears. In reality it is not blowing that hard. If we stop paddling we won't lose too much ground. But there is something about a headwind that instills a feeling of struggle, like mild desperation. Everyone is working hard and we may even be going much faster than we had been before, when we were waylaid by the allure of Sulphur Passage. Now, our focus is to reach the southwestern part of Obstruction Island and cross over Hayden Passage. Once we reach Flores Island we will be able to tuck in along the shore and hide from the wind.

The sudden seriousness is a good thing. It is important to be reminded of the challenges kayakers need to be prepared for. So far on this trip we have been lulled by gentle conditions, and have used our bodies constantly, but gently. We have not even begun to see the extent to which we can push ourselves if necessary.

It shouldn't be too difficult to meter our strength across the next section. We had planned to have lunch at Riley Cove, a bay on the northwestern tip of Flores Island, but that might have to be reconsidered; we might need to stop sooner, perhaps at Steamer Cove. As we near Hayden Passage the wind drops slightly, but the chop from the ebbing tide is more noticeable. Although it disturbs the surface conditions, the tide does benefit us, and at one point we can definitely feel its force, pulling us along.

The crossing is not too difficult, but the energy of the group is obviously beginning to wane. A welcome distraction comes in the form of a black bear near a creek on Flores. The distraction is even more entertaining when Adrian's binoculars show us that the bear is, in fact, a large rock. How many large round rocks have been mistaken for black bears in the past? I'm almost embarrassed to count my own blunders. Each time I see one of those rocks I assume that experience has made me smarter, more able to differentiate. But no. . . .

Not far from here, one researcher spent several summers differentiating between

Sydney Inlet: a study in light and motion. When the water dances, the kayaks seem to dance too. In this case, they're dancing toward the northwestern shore of Flores Island.

large round rocks and black bears. Clio Island lies across the water from us, near a rocky beach on the mainland that is heavily used by black bears. The Clayoquot Biosphere Project built a research platform on this island, overlooking the beach. The black bears in Clayoquot Sound make heavy use of intertidal areas for food. When the tide is low, and especially in spring when they are hungry, the bears wander the shoreline, turning over rocks in their search for crabs. At these times, people on the water can observe the bears without disturbing them; in fact, the bears can be quite hard to disturb. Sometimes they appear oblivious to everything but the closest and noisiest of motorboats, completely absorbed in their search for food.

Easy to watch, these bears are also easy to shoot. Trophy hunters need only a gun, a licence and a boat. Courage and skill are secondary. After taking the head and the hide, they are allowed to take only a fraction of the animal as meat and leave the rest of the carcass on the beach to rot. The practice reveals a gory truth about the excessiveness of society.

In 1988 a handful of people from Tofino attempted to prevent an outfitter from arranging bear kills for his clients. Using small open boats, they ran interference between the hunters and the bears. The situation quickly got out of hand and eventually arrests were made. Four years later the situation flared up again. A bear was shot and skinned. In the ensuing fracas, one of the protestors made off with the hide, intending for it to remain in the sound, not on a wall somewhere in the United States. Again, more people were arrested.

The following year, vigilant bear protectors monitored the beaches of the sound during each low tide, covering large distances by boat. That year the dispute centred around a local hunter. Again a black bear was killed; again only the hide and head were taken. The issue reached a climax when someone retrieved the headless, skinless carcass of the bear and displayed it for all to see, first at the village green in Tofino and later in front of the legislature buildings in Victoria. As a tool for educating the public it was brutally effective, provoking calls for a ban on the trophy hunting of bears.

In recent years there has been a slackening of the tension, although the situation has by no means been resolved. Meanwhile the charter boat industry has adopted bear watching as a tour option. Boats lingering near Clio Island are more likely to contain humans with cameras now, not humans with guns.

Bear watching would be a pleasant diversion this morning, but getting back and forth to Clio Island means crossing Shelter Inlet twice, which is not realistic given the wind. Already the pace of the group has slowed considerably and we seem to be taking a long time to reach Flores Island. Eventually we pause under a lofty Douglas fir to reassess the situation. We obviously need a rest, preferably fairly soon, and since the nearest beach is in Steamer Cove, the decision to stop there is easily made. The anticipation of an imminent break helps boost the waning morale and propels us onwards once again.

I had hoped to avoid stopping in Steamer Cove, because of the scenery. It must have been beautiful here before it was clearcut. Now the hillside is littered with roads and stumps and rusting logging equipment. I'm not surprised that the waters below the clearcut are adorned with a fish farm – the two activities seem intrinsically linked.

Rather than stopping on a beach that is edged by slash, we sneak in amongst the George Islands, where the sight of the destroyed hillside is more easily avoided. Our lunching islet is redeemed by strange boulders, erratically placed and covered with moss. Even at some distance from the beach, the water is rocky and shallow, hinting that the area will soon be exposed by the ebbing tide. We unload necessities and while Jan lays out the picnic I wade the boats over to deeper water, pulling them along with ease, happy to know that we won't be lifting them later.

The sand is soft and slightly muddy, a perfect environment for clams. The bay used to be a temporary camp for Native clam diggers; in fact, there is even a canoe run still visible in the northwestern part of the cove. Canoe runs are conspicuous because of the parallel lines of boulders on either side of them. Swathes of smooth gravel that transect rocky beaches, they were used for the launching and landing of the dugouts. Unlike structures made of wood, the rocks' weight and permanence ensured that they would be one of the more lasting indicators of historical use. The buildings that were used here were neither lasting nor permanent. The clam diggers fixed cedar-bark mats to wooden frameworks and called these places home until a plentiful supply of butter clams had been dug and preserved for the winter.

Compared to other species, butter clams are fairly large. Most commercial varieties are smaller, with the exception of geoducks – huge deepwater clams that are sold for a fortune in Japan. Few people harvest butter clams anymore, but they are tasty – great for clam burgers. Their drawback is the length of time that they can be affected by red tide, caused by toxic phytoplankton blooming in warm water. Clams ingest this toxin as they feed and are unaffected by it, but when humans or other mammals consume the clams, paralytic shellfish poisoning can result. Butter clams can retain traces of the poison for up to two years, although its effect may be milder the longer the poison has been in the clam.

During severe blooms of red tide, the Department of Fisheries will usually announce the closure of contaminated beaches. Determined shellfish eaters should advise themselves well before departing on a trip. A potful of clams can be delightful, as long as the diners survive. My own policy is to collect shellfish after the first frost and through the winter and spring, by which time – if I have been diligent enough – my cravings are usually satiated and I can survive the summer without them. Having said that, I give the smoked oysters at lunch a substantial amount of my attention.

Our break does not involve a lot of exploration. We can't afford much time, so the focus is on refueling and relaxing, recovering from the tiring morning and preparing for the long afternoon. Now that we have reached Flores, we can see that we will be able to avoid much of the wind by sticking close to shore until we get to Riley Cove. Essentially the afternoon can be divided into two parts: the first half, partially protected from the wind; the second half, exposed to the wind, the tide and the swell. When our batteries are finally topped up, we squelch across the mud to the boats. They are perfectly positioned, the water having receded just enough to make packing and launching uncomplicated.

Straight away we head for the main part of Flores, passing the old canoe run as we go, glad to see evidence of manual forms of travel. Amongst the subtle lines of nature, the angularity of this construction is almost jarring, yet canoe runs often pass unobserved. They are one of the least noticed of cultural markers.

This morning's paddle has demonstrated the need for a steady pace and has given us a better idea of the amount of energy that we might need to expend later on. We reach Riley Cove with little difficulty, stopping only briefly to prepare for the wind that we are likely to face after rounding Starling Point. Luckily, the conditions don't turn out to be too bad. The tide and the wind are coming our way, which means that we will have to paddle against them both, but the surface water will be smoother, with fewer whitecaps. This area is more exposed to the ocean, bouncier than the inlets we have grown accustomed to lately. Despite the added work, it is exhilarating to leave the inlets behind and feel the power of the swell.

Once again, determination knots our paddling faces, and conversation lags. The noise of the wind precludes idle chatter; besides, it is distracting to talk when so much needs to be accomplished. As before, the more noticeable the wind, the faster our pace. I have a hunch that we might even be clocking our fastest time yet, although I have little to compare it to. Our routes have been so indirect and varied on this trip that we haven't really established an average cruising speed.

After a while, we stop at a creek for water and are unable to resist shaking off some of the hard work with a swim. We are actually quite close to the beach that is our intended destination at this point and the break is timely. We have cruised into an area that is sheltered, but once we round the next point the effects of the wind and the swell will require extra strength and attention. We are near the end of a long day and the refreshingly cold water perks us up, giving us an extra shot of enthusiasm for the final 15 minutes.

Sure enough, the last stretch of water rolls and heaves under and over the boats, throwing white, salty splashes across our arms and faces. That I never seem to

The last supper is tinged with all the solemnity appropriate for such an occasion, but is also filled with colour, as a combination of marinated beets and carrots mimics the intense hues of the western sky.

approach this beach in any other weather is a thought that makes me smile as the rocky stacks loom up ahead. Once past these barriers we will be in a crescent-shaped, possibly sheltered bay, but until then, some watchfulness is called for. I gesture towards the more dangerous areas, but the need for caution requires few words.

We land with great relief and a satisfying sense of accomplishment. Despite the distance and all the work, we have actually arrived a few hours before sunset, which must be a record for this trip. Not only will we have plenty of time to set up camp and cook dinner, there might even be a few minutes for some solitude, an opportunity to shut off all the systems and close down. I put this at the top of my mental list of priorities. Right now I am unpacking, thanking the kayak for its seaworthiness as I do so. There is little so depressing as opening up a hatch to find the compartment full of water and half of the gear soaked through. The bulkheads in my kayak are separated from the cockpit by watertight dividing walls. They can be accessed through openings in the front and rear and are sealed by a combination of closures. A soft neoprene cover fits snugly over each opening; a fibreglass lid fits on top of the neoprene, protecting it and maintaining the integrity of the deck. The weak link in the system is the soft cover. It's so simple to put down a piece of neoprene while unpacking and forget about it, only to find out later that the tide has swept it away. Neoprene is also susceptible to the effects of salt water, becoming easily worn at the seams. The soft neoprene hatch is the waterproof component, and needs to be well maintained for safety's sake.

As well as dry storage areas, the bulkheads provide buoyancy, a vital element in any boat. The most polished Eskimo rolls and rescue techniques will have little effect in a kayak that is filling up with water and going under – an unwelcome event that does happen. An accident in the Queen Charlotte Islands several years ago began with a sunken boat and grew progressively worse. At the end of a long day, one of the participants on the trip capsized in heavy seas. The paddler was rescued, but capsized again soon afterwards; this time things were different, this time the kayak sank. Water in the Queen Charlotte Islands is painfully cold and hypothermia quickly made the situation critical. The paddler was draped over the back of a double kayak and immediately taken to land, but the perilous shoreline precluded the option of landing the entire group. In the space of time it took to find an alternative landing site, two more paddlers capsized, one of whom drowned.

In this incident the boat sank because a rubber seal had been lost, which let water from the seating area into both bulkheads. The leak could have been detected earlier. On land, over short or long distances, the temptation to drag kayaks is hard to resist, with the result being that the most scratched part of any kayak is usually the stern, as the front is lifted to drag the boat, and weight and stress are concentrated on the back. Leaks eventually develop, but when the fore and aft bulkheads are designed to be completely separate from one another, the leak can be confined to a single compartment, making it easier to deal with. Some leaks can be temporarily bandaged with duct tape, but a kayak should not be considered seaworthy unless a repair job has been well proven.

I am always relieved to find my hatches dry after a drenching paddle, although now, looking at the hull of my boat, I can see that the gel coat will soon need another application. I chalk up the job as yet another winter project and wait for help before carrying the boats up to the logs and tying them off. Sometimes I feel silly tying the boats when they are so far from the water, but I know how much sillier I would feel if a freak wave carried them away at high tide in the middle of the night.

This beach has many names; in fact, it has so many names that I sometimes have to point it out on the chart before people know which one I am talking about. Some know it as Half Moon Bay, but there is also a beach near Ucluelet with this name. The people from Hotsprings Cove call it Sandy Beach, while others refer to it as Ann's beach. Crazy Eagle Beach is another name for it – perhaps because of the strange antics of a local pair of eagles.

From the water, it is hard to tell that there is a beach here at all. The entrance is protectively ringed by rocky stacks, keeping out the onslaught of the sea. On shore, sand curves around the water like a sickle, enhancing the prettiness. The swell, crashing against the rocks, is diluted, and becomes tiers of frothy surf that make landing manageable. Landing is not always manageable, however; this is not a place to trifle with when the swell is up or a storm is brewing, which is obvious from the variety of jetsam on the beach. Aside from the usual accumulation of logs, I usually find something interesting here. This evening my eye fixes immediately on a worn piece of wood, covered in spirals and swirls. It is similar to a burl, but I suspect that it is part of a root. It is about two and a half feet long and heavier on one end, like a baseball bat. I have no idea what it would be useful for, but the magpie in me wants to keep it. It is heavy, though, and could require some creative packing. Perhaps I'll have to leave it behind after all.

I tuck my prize behind a log and continue aimlessly down the beach. The idea of walking barefoot on the sand entices me, but if I want to find a Japanese glass ball I will have to check among the logs. I keep my sandals on and browse amidst the drift-wood chaos that many European visitors find so distressingly untidy. Glass balls are rare these days; since most Japanese fishermen now use plastic floats for their nets the supply has been sadly depleted. I have only ever found one Japanese glass ball, a small green one that washed up on Long Beach in February many years ago. At the moment of my discovery, onlookers would not have been far wrong in assuming that I had won the lottery. It certainly felt that way to me. The fact that this little piece of glass had floated across the ocean from Japan and washed up safely at my feet involved tremendous odds. I was deliriously happy, having wanted to find one for ages.

That small scratched piece of glass was one of my most treasured possessions until the day it left me. At the time, I was in the process of moving house and some friends were helping me carry boxes down to the dock. A week later they remembered to tell me that "one of those glass balls of yours fell out of a box into the water." They said they had been going to retrieve it, but by the time they got down to the dock it had floated out of sight. Of course I pointed out that this was in fact the *only* glass ball that I had ever found in my entire life, but in a way the ending was appropriate. It floated out of my life and – I hope – floated into someone else's. I always wonder where it came from and where it has ended up. Maybe there's a chance that I will find it again. Who knows? It could be under one of these huge logs.

The beach is strewn with small chunks of dry cedar, perfect for a fire. I fill up my arms before returning to camp and find that I have not been alone in collecting pieces of wood. On his wanderings Adrian has come across the stern piece of a dugout canoe. It is not some ancient artifact, but part of a canoe that was made a few years ago. The black paint has weathered its journey well.

There has been a resurgence in canoe making among the Nuu-chah-nulth in recent years and one family from the Tla-o-qui-aht band, the Martins, have been responsible for carving a number of dugouts. This piece must be from one of their canoes and I wonder how it ended up here. In a dugout, the prow and stern pieces are created separately and fitted onto the main body of the dugout afterwards. The elegant prow resembles the neck and head of a deer, while the stern is less elaborate, rising up at right angles to the boat, deflecting any waves that might come from behind.

In 1997 the Nuu-chah-nulth reconnected with their relatives on the other side of the border by paddling to Port Angeles, Neah Bay and La Push in a fantastic tribal journey. They stayed a few days in each place, feasting and meeting distant family members before paddling back across the Strait of Juan de Fuca. The Tla-o-qui-aht canoe made the return journey in 33 hours, encountering heavy fog along the way. The Martins were pleased with the performance of their canoes, which illustrated the effectiveness of the old designs.

In 1999 a canoe festival is being planned by the Ahousaht, a huge event, one that reflects the importance that is being attached to the revival of traditional connections. This stern piece may be needed on its canoe for that celebration, and we debate the merits of bringing it with us, but it is too big to fit in one of the holds and would be awkward to strap on deck. We decide to put it somewhere safe and let the carvers know its whereabouts.

Meanwhile Jan and I devote extra attention to the details of this evening's banquet. Even though we are near the end of the trip, we still have a variety of fresh food, and our marinaded salad of carrots, beets and chick peas rivals the colour of the sunset. Combined with an outrageously lavish creation of pesto pasta, the meal feels decadent enough to be worthy of such accomplished paddlers. Of course, there is also chocolate afterwards, which we devour in sickening quantities around the fire. Clouds have crept into the sky, hinting at the front that was forecast this morning, but we are out of radio reception here and despite my cajoling, the weather channel picks up nothing but static. We will have to wait and see what the morning brings us.

This evening the fire takes on a life of its own, a little heap of coals pulsing its corona of warmth out into the blackness. I become truly mesmerized, staring until late into the night. The week's adventures are eddying around me, brought closer by the darkening tunnel of the night. Inhaling deeply, I try to fill every nook and cranny with this surfeit of pleasure, to expand the space onto which these experiences can be imprinted. Eyes glazed, I crouch over, hugging my knees and wishing that the end were not so near.

Few things reward the achievement of a hard-won journey as well as a sunset. In this case it is a luxury to have arrived safely and to know that good food and warm sleeping bags are waiting for us.

Chapter Seven
WINDING DOWN

From Crazy Eagle Beach, Flores Island
to Tofino via the Matlahaw

T'S LUCKY THAT TODAY'S PLANS DO NOT INVOLVE ANY URGENCY, because our usual rising time passes unnoticed. When we finally venture out into the morning light, we are still weary from yesterday's exertions – movements languid, voices quiet. In between patches of sunlight, clouds smudge the beach with cool shadows. I start the fire again, deciding to try a different approach to pancake making. This time I am determined to create the perfect source of heat, although I will still have to deal with the inadequate frying pan. When the fire is established, I gradually add some small chunks of bark gleaned from the tideline. A Tla-o-qui-aht man once told me that his grandmother preferred to use pieces of bark for her cooking fires because of the slow, even heat they produce. This is precisely the outcome I am looking for. I dice an apple finely, then boil some water to rehydrate a fistful of dried cranberries from the Marktosis Grocery. I'm hoping that a hearty breakfast will provide sufficient distraction from the aching muscles and lingering sleepiness.

Despite their apparent starkness, the rocky islands near Crazy Eagle Beach are home
to a profusion of hardy plants such as this Nootka Rose. Normally these roses bloom
in June, but this flower still looks vibrant in the first week of July.

The heat is perfect, eliciting the required bubbles from each panful of batter without burning. A warm bowl by the fireside fills with successive batches until it threatens to overflow, at which point – saturated with melted butter and honey – the pancakes are rapaciously devoured, accompanied by calls for more. The mood of the group becomes cheery and slightly more energetic, but only slightly.

Overtiredness can spawn irritability, so the success of a trip hinges on the need for breaks, to allow people time to replenish their supply of energy. Sometimes an hour of daily time out is all that's required, but if the need is consistently overlooked, the problem can be manifested in inappropriate behaviour, usually at times of crisis, when rational thinking is critical. Assessing levels of tiredness among leaders and participants is part of a formula for successful expeditions. Even though we are so close to the end of the trip, it would be counterproductive to rush anywhere this morning unless we absolutely have to.

Sun and clouds continue to take turns dominating the sky and there is a light wind coming from the south. We are still out of radio reception, nestled behind the mountains of Flores Island. I am curious about the wind, wondering if it is going to increase. Our plans for the day are loose and involve only two aspirations: a soak in the hot springs and a water-taxi ride to Tofino. If the wind is going to be strong, we should head over to Openit Peninsula right away, so that we can round Sharp Point while the conditions are still good. Once we are in Hotsprings Cove the issue of weather will be less important; the kayaking will be over. If the wind is going to remain calm, however, it would be great to stay right where we are and postpone our reacquaintance with civilization, extending the wilderness portion of the day. Besides, this beach has attained an almost iconic significance as the goal of all yesterday's hard work. It would be a shame to rush away from it.

I decide to paddle out into Sydney Inlet to see if the open water will provide a better environment for radio reception. A few hundred yards from the beach there is no improvement, so I continue across the inlet for about another half-mile. Still no luck, although the radio seems to be working because I can pick up transmissions from the whale-watching fraternity. But I am not interested in hearing why the whale at Siwash Cove is being so elusive; I want the marine forecast. I try contacting one of the boats, hoping they can relay the forecast, but my calls go unanswered. Perhaps the batteries are low. Giving it up as a bad job, I paddle over to a sport-fishing boat by the far shore. The boat looks fancy and I am confident that it will be equipped with a battery of electronic gadgets. I can see two people on the boat – a man and a boy. Just as I draw near, the man hooks onto a fish. Eventually, it breaks the surface, flinging out sprays of water in violent resistance. It turns out to be a large dogfish. As I watch the resulting chaos, I can see that if I ever catch one of these from a kayak I will have no choice but to cut the line. After repeated attempts to unhook the dogfish, the man is finally successful. At my request, the man turns up the VHF and tunes it to the weather channel. That done, he continues fishing, completely ignoring my presence, exuding taciturn vibes. He has done me a favour, however, so I thank him for his time before paddling back across the inlet.

The forecast expects moderate, variable winds today with an outlook for moderate northwesterlies tomorrow. We seem to be in a lull between systems, which can mean fine weather for paddling. It also means that we don't have rush away from Flores, so I decide to stay out a little longer and go fishing. The rocks outside the entrance to the beach seem a likely place for jigging, but when nothing responds to my lure, I decide to try further out, at the next set of rocks. The swell has increased noticeably today and the exposure keeps me on my toes. Once or twice an extra-large wave rolls underneath the boat while I am concentrating on the rod and line, surprising me and warning me to pay attention. Close by, lying plumply on a low rock between two seastacks, a harbour seal is trying to sunbathe. The location seems perilous, hardly an ideal place to relax. From time to time the seal is obliterated from view by a crash of whitewater, somehow always managing to retain its position and its accompanying air of nonchalance.

One's patience for fishing can be eroded very quickly when one catches nothing but seaweed and rocks. When I finally do catch a fish, it is depressingly small – a tiddler with lots of ambition and no concept of size. The fish is only slightly bigger than my lure. How did it open its mouth wide enough to bite the hook? Slightly disgusted, I head back to camp, realizing how far I have travelled this morning without intending to.

Returning to the beach, I see Adrian taking photos on one of the islands. He must have hopped across the large boulders when the tide was low enough. Jan is motionless, blissfully soaking up the sun at the far end of the beach. The sky has cleared, the sun finally outcompeting the clouds. I marvel at our continued good fortune with the weather. I had half-expected that by this stage of the trip we would be cold and soggy and clamouring to return home. Instead, we will have to pry ourselves away, like oysters from a rock.

The Last Lunch does not share the éclat of the Last Supper or the Last Breakfast. There is something about lunch materials that does not always weather well. Stale tortillas crumble the moment they are touched; crackers bend instead of breaking; bags of sprouts can be mistaken for compost. The meal is redeemed by some of the leftovers from last night and a precious can of sockeye salmon. And of course, since there is so much chocolate left over, it would be wasteful not to consume it, although we should leave a little for emergencies.

After lunch, the packing proceeds unhurriedly; our reluctance to leave is obvious. The process is absorbing, however, and helps move our minds to the fun that still lies ahead. By the time we are ready, the prospect of a dip in the hot springs leads us down the beach and into our boats. The launch goes smoothly, although the increase in swell is reflected in the size of the surf. Launching in surf is mostly a matter of patience. Careful watching, over time, will reveal the patterns of movement. Often a number of big waves will arrive one after another, but the group may then be followed by a relatively calm patch. The two usually alternate in a fairly regular pattern.

Lunch at Crazy Eagle beach, Flores Island. Despite the fact that it is day seven, our lunch menu is still edible and varied. But not for much longer…

Getting to know the pattern of the day is a kayaker's ticket to getting off the beach, although the best-laid plans can always be thwarted by an unexpected wave, the one that preferred to travel alone.

When encountering breaking waves, the best approach is head on, paddling like stink, keeping the boat perpendicular to the wave. If you allow the wave to break before you reach it, its strength will be diminished, making paddling through it easier. If the wave is building as you approach and you get there before it breaks, some adrenaline-pumped sprinting is usually effective. The most agonizing moment is when you realize that whatever you do, the wave is going to break right on top of you. At that point, the best thing to do is hang on and keep paddling. It can go both ways. There have been occasions when I've squeaked through, against the odds, and other times when the massive force of the breaking wave has spat me back to shore, tumbling all the way.

The surf on the beach today is the variety that usually only produces minor incidents – a lapful of water or a broached boat that needs to be relaunched. We exit smoothly, still sad to be leaving. Once we're in Sydney Inlet, however, the paddling conditions are superb and the motion is infectious. It seems to take only minutes for us to reach the other side. For reasons of variety we have decided to land on the east side of Openit Peninsula, at a small beach from which we can access the main boardwalk leading to the springs. Because of the broken radio we have not arranged this evening's water-taxi ride. It would be infinitely more sensible to paddle around the peninsula and look for boats at the government dock, but we decide to leave this mundane matter in the hands of serendipity.

We have landed on traditional Manhousaht territory, close to the site of what was once a well-fortified village. The Manhousaht lands extended inland from the region of the hot springs, then on down the coast of Flores Island to Siwash Cove, where the tribe shared their southern border with the O-tsus-aht. It's hardly surprising that the village on this peninsula was fortified; the hot springs must have been a highly coveted prize, capable of inciting territorial jealousies. Above the high-tide line, the rambling growth of berry bushes hints at a clearing that must once have existed here. By the 1940s there were so few Manhousaht left alive that they abandoned this treasured place to join forces with the Ahousaht.

The profusion of growth gives the sense that this site has not been visited by humans recently, a suspicion which increases when the entrance to the trail proves difficult to find. When we finally locate it, we find the first section so overgrown that it has become a tunnel. We crouch down and beat our way through it until the berries gradually turn to forest and the going improves. We are crossing the peninsula now, heading west to the main trail, which runs parallel to the shoreline. This is not a well-advertised route; we are walking on the forest floor – and occasionally through deep mud – as opposed to being swept along on a boardwalk. I enjoy the comparative quietness of stepping on soft earth and the meandering twists and turns of the path-way. At one point, a pair of fantastically corkscrewed cedars rise up on either side of the path like sentries. Moss grows like a green ribbon in the grooves of one tree's spi-ral, etching its deformity in colour. We ponder the natural forces that would produce such bizarrely shaped trees, but come up with little that resembles a cogent theory.

Suddenly, we break out of the forest and onto the boardwalk. We feel like coun-try mice come to town! The new boardwalk is so extravagant that it feels like a reg-ular highway. All it needs now are some yellow lines and a passing lane. When I first came to the hot springs, nine years ago, the trail was longer and more convoluted, but it had more character than it does now. Many of the hand-split boards had the names of people or boats carved into them, often artistically and with obvious care. This tradition is tentatively reestablishing itself along the new boardwalk – a link between the old and the new. As part of Maquinna Provincial Park, the construction of the trail must uphold specific requirements. There is a tremendous increase in tours to the hot springs and, realistically, this trail now needs to be strong and safe. Some of the people we encounter along on the trail look as if they have never stepped off a sidewalk in their lives.

The most noticeable thing about the tourists is their smell. We've been removed from artificial environments for seven days, and the wafting stink of aftershave is offensive to all of us; our delicate olfactory systems are easily assailed. Perfume seems so contrary to the notion of purity that is associated with hot springs. Perhaps I am being unjustly superior; after all, eau-de-campfire is also a powerful scent – the tourists could probably smell us a mile away, too. Most likely, I am simply reacting with irritation to the unavoidable proximity of civilization.

All the people we meet on the trail are heading toward the government dock, indicating that a boat is due to leave soon. Optimistically, I dare to hope that the springs will be empty when we get there. It would be too overwhelming to find the rocks teeming with people and the pools full of bodies. I have grown fussy about my visits to the hot springs recently, trying to choose the less busy times of the day, of the week, of the year, so that I won't have to share the experience with strangers. The more people we pass, the more optimistic I become, almost skipping with anticipation.

Just before we reach the springs we run into a small group of people from Hotsprings Village. Two of the women are longtime acquaintances of mine and we are happy to catch up with each other's news. It is a fortuitous meeting: Paula's husband, Clifford, skippers the *Matlahaw*, the Native water taxi that zooms back and forth from the cove to Tofino several times a day. It turns out that there will be room on the boat later this evening, which allows us just the right amount of time to soak, hike and paddle around the point into the cove. Having left the booking of the water taxi to chance, I am relieved at this smooth outcome. If we had been unable to find a boat this evening, we would have had to stay overnight at the Maquinna Park campground and waited until tomorrow to get a place on a boat, which would have added another day to the trip. Now we will return on schedule, according to our route plan. And we won't have to eat rehydrated carrots and lentils with soggy crackers tonight.

I shake my head in mild disbelief at the luck of the encounter. As Paula's group heads back to the village, we comment on how lucky they are to be able to visit the springs whenever the desire strikes. I'm also reassured to see locals here – the springs have not become exclusively a tourist attraction.

Along with the new trail, an elaborate wooden landing has been constructed to announce the moment of arrival at the hot springs at Sharp Point. The landing displays a large, detailed sign that outlines the scientific reasons behind the upwelling of hot water. Sharp Point is described as being situated along a geological fault. Surface water apparently flows through the fault to a depth of five kilometres, where it is geothermally heated to 109 degrees Celsius before being hydrostatically forced back up to the surface again. Once at the surface, the heated water exits through rocky fissures at a flow rate of five to eight litres per second. Fortunately for bathers, the temperature here is 109 degrees; it has cooled to about 50 degrees, which – when mixed with the chilly Pacific in a rocky pool at high tide – is usually just a little hotter than most people's baths.

I am intrigued by the location of the fault. It seems to extend for miles, even up to Hesquiaht Lake and I wonder if it also transects Sydney Inlet. The distinctive islets at Crazy Eagle Beach seem so different from the surrounding rocks. Could it be that they are part of the same fault? Imagine a little hot pool over there. . . .

Right now, however, we don't need to imagine anything. We are above the hot pools, at the actual source. The water surfaces from its mysterious underworld in a stream of tiny bubbles and flows along a narrow channel draped with pale grey algae, as if it is a creation of fantasy – something out of *The Hobbit*. Tendrils of sulphurous mist swirl above the waterway, enhancing the storybook feel. Further on, the water flows under the graceful root of a hemlock tree – a beautiful bridge over a strange stream. All that is missing from the picture is a scattering of fairies and elves. But maybe they are not missing.

I am glad to see that the old clawfoot enamel bathtub is still here. Thankfully, no one has decided to "tidy up" this ornament. The tub has been here for years, and although it receives a steady supply of hot water, few people actually bathe in it. There is something quite surreal about the bathtub's presence. It would be sad if anyone removed it; it is the only physical pointer to the fact that these springs have a history of use by locals and fishermen, that they weren't always just part of a tour.

Victory! We have reached our destination! But, sinking into a steaming pool, we soon discover the areas that are the most sunburned. Luckily, an ice cold tide pool – the other extreme – waits for us nearby.

Excited now, we run down the stairway to see if there are any other bathers. The hot water flows over a lip of rock, dropping about 12 feet into a pool. There is no one under the waterfall. Staying below the height of rock, the stream meanders towards the ocean, forming several small pools along the way. There are no people in the middle pools. The pools become progressively cooler as they approach the sea; they are often flooded by the high tide. Their comfortable temperature makes the lower pools the most popular. There is no one in the lower pools.

There is no one on the surrounding rocks.

There is no one here at all!

We throw off our clothes and hurry down to test the water temperature. Sinking into one of the middle pools, I soon find out where I am most sunburned – my fore-arms, from this morning's fishing. The heat is searing; the pool is made even hotter by the afternoon sun. Jan and I quickly seek the relief of the icy, salt water tide pools just below the springs, where – along with mussels, barnacles and sea anemones – we await the next surge of swell. When we're cool enough we venture back for another hot soak, this time more appreciative of the heat, perhaps slightly numbed by the cold! Eventually, it becomes time to cool off again and we revisit the ocean pools, even though they are quickly being covered over by the rising tide. By this stage, the hot-cold immersion has produced the desired effect on my body. Not wanting to overdo the feeling, I finish off with one last blast of heat from the waterfall, and head up to the rocks to sit in the sun and dry off.

The best time to experience the waterfall is in midwinter. Once, in January, when there was snow on the ground, I draped myself over the boulder that is so strategically placed beneath the hot cascade. The rainy winter weather had cooled the water to a perfect temperature and the resulting massage was almost impossible to drag myself away from. Since then, I always test out the waterfall, but have never recaptured the perfection of that moment.

As we sit on the rocks overlooking the cove, I imagine myself as the person who first discovered these springs. Would I have tested the water, or would I have been afraid of its magical power? All the factual explanations in the world cannot detract from the sense of mystery that the hot bubbling springs provoke. Perhaps the find would have elevated my status in society. Regardless, the moment of discovery must have been pivotal, unforgettable.

The afternoon sun is throwing sparkles across the water in a mesmerizing kaleidescope. We stare dreamily out to sea, temporarily drained of energy, but imbued with a companionable glow. Chatting peacefully about this and that, we try to gather the strength and willpower to move, an achievement that seems to take some time. In the end, incentive is provided by the arrival of a young couple, both of whom light cigarettes. The smoke wafts up to our rocky perch and quickly sets us on our feet, ready to go.

Each of us has chosen a trailside feature as a marker to denote the turnoff from the boardwalk. The little trail meets the boardwalk in a bushy profusion of salal and the entrance could be easily missed, but with all of us paying attention we find it right away. Two dogs have accompanied us, despite our best efforts to deter them. I suspect they are from Hotsprings Village and are accustomed to roaming free. They seem delighted to be on this new path and bound on cheerfully ahead. The three of us spread out along the trail, each moving at our own pace, each wanting to savour these last few drops of time.

Back at the boats, we find the light has softened. To the north, Holmes Inlet is a blur of subtle greens. To the south, a band of fog is slowly approaching, the first wisps curling around the treeline on Flores. We paddle easily down the length of the peninsula toward Sharp Point, noticing an increase in wind, which may be associated with the fog. It will be good to get around the point before the fog comes in.

Sharp Point is renowned for its ferocious conditions. Openit Peninsula is sandwiched between two inlets, one of which, the Sydney, carries vast quantities of water with the pull of every tide. The peninsula is also completely exposed to the onslaught of the ocean. No barriers soften the blow of the waves. Stuck between this combination of powerful and often conflicting forces, Sharp Point pokes out to sea – its rocky teeth frequently the site of a roiling mass of confusion and whitewater. In the middle of winter, when storms pound the coast and the roar of the swell can be heard even from the inlets, I think of the children from the village, rounding this point in the *Matlahaw* on their way down the coast to school. The skippers from this village are some of the most experienced on the coast; theirs is a brutal immersion in the ways of the sea.

For kayakers, Sharp Point is best travelled in conditions of absolute calm. Today, we are not so lucky and find ourselves in a messy pitch of steep chop – each wave heralding from a different direction. The water slaps our boats around with quick blows, keeping us alert; we keep our legs firmly braced to maximize our stability. Conflicting currents meet and swirl; occasional breakers wash over our laps. The need for intense concentration is exhilarating and there is pleasure in focusing the senses so acutely. The challenge diminishes as we head into the cove, although the swell now comes at us from behind and it is still necessary to concentrate to avoid any unexpected surprises. A boat drones slowly past us, thrumming a deep diesel tone, heading for the government dock on the eastern side of the cove. From the 1930s until the late 1960s this was the site of a marine service station and store. It was also possible for fishermen to sell their catch here, but eventually, Maquinna Provincial Park preempted land from which to access the hot springs. The government dock now marks the start of the boardwalk. In recent years a tiny store-cum-information kiosk has been constructed near the dock, along with a handful of campsites.

Hotsprings Cove is a simple inlet with few curves or bends. At the end of the inlet the lowlands quickly crawl up the side of a mountain. A river spills out into the salt water and a pale green patch of alders hint at some recent disturbance here. The

Trademark red railings identify this as the government wharf at Maquinna Provincial Park, Hotsprings Cove. The feet that climb this ramp will be in for a treat when they reach the hot springs and are immersed in soothing water.

present site of Hotsprings Village is along the sloping west side of the inlet – not a typical location for a Native village. The original site was here, at the head of the inlet. It was well chosen for most things, with one noticeable exception: it lay directly in the path of the tsunami of 1964. That was the year of the Good Friday earthquake in Alaska, which sent a giant wave rolling down the coast, devastating some places and leaving others untouched. Tofino was little affected, but the town of Port Alberni – lying at the head of a long inlet – experienced heavy damage. Hotsprings Village was at the end of a short straight inlet, perfectly designed for funnelling the wave and causing the water to slap up against the end of the bay. Some houses floated completely away, others were moved off their foundations. The new village draws on the lessons of the old one and is situated partway down the inlet, where the waters are still protected enough to allow safe moorage. The houses are built on a steep slope, giving them the immediate advantage of elevation. For a seagoing people, however, the idea of building a community away from the water entirely is out of the question.

Despite the fact that these are the traditional lands of the Manhousaht, the people who live at Hotsprings Cove are the Hesquiaht, whose own lands lie to the northwest, along the shores of the harbour at Hesquiaht and out toward Estevan Point. The reason for their relocation was the same old story: scant numbers and centralization. The cove was a centre because of the marine store and fish-buying facility, but the Hesquiaht have not forgotten their traditional lands. On the contrary, they are a united group of people, with a great vision for the future and a strongly independent spirit. In guardianship of their territory they have initiated the Project for the Management of a Living Hesquiaht Harbour. Through this project they have applied their own brand of management to the use of the resources within the harbour, especially the fisheries. Their vision is one of great magnitude: they use the life span of a cedar tree as the time frame over which planning should take place. Chief Councillor Steve Charleson hopes that 2,000 years in the future the Hesquiaht will be able to eat the same foods, in the same quantities, as they did when he was a child. He is determined that his own children maintain a strong connection with the land, that they always know how and where to find food.

The impression of unity the Hesquiaht make may derive from their comparative isolation. The lengthy days of winter lend themselves to social gatherings, along with all the associated activities: dancing, singing, making costumes, preparing food. The elementary school here has a strong cultural program and teaches the basics of the language, as well as other skills. This is not to say that the influence of Western culture is not apparent here; it is, but it seems to have become part of a tapestry, blending with some aspects of life without subtracting from a sense of cultural integrity.

Hotsprings Village always has a nice feel to it, a languid atmosphere that spreads itself outwards. We arrive at the dock with half an hour to spare, which is perfect; the extra time allows us to empty all our gear into a heap on the dock and stuff our myriad small bags into a handful of larger duffels. The boats should be empty for transportation; anything left in their hulls could bang around and cause damage. Also, we will have to lift the boats on and off the cabin of the *Matlahaw*, for which purpose it will be best to have them as light as possible. Kayaks often sustain much of their accumulated damage through the various processes of mechanical transportation – on the roof racks of cars, on the pontoons of float planes, on the cabins of boats . . .

While we're waiting for the boat, we are joined by a number of fellow travellers and the mood quickly becomes jovial. Several babies make their way around the group – passed from one admirer to the next – enjoying every moment of attention. A gathering in Ahousaht is attracting some of the people, while others will be coming all the way into Tofino with us. When the boat has refuelled, we strap two of the kayaks onto the roof of the cabin, resting the third crosswise on the rear railings of the boat. Life jackets and spray skirts are sandwiched in every possible space between the *Matlahaw*'s aluminum and the kayaks' fibreglass. We need as much padding as we can find because the wind has picked up and the sea conditions have deteriorated.

Because Ahousaht is one of our stops on this trip, we will be travelling on the inside of Flores, retracing our paddle strokes. I had hoped that we would return on the outside of Flores, which would make our journey circular. The outer route involves a spectacular stretch of coastline – extremely dangerous and exposed but breathtaking in its ruggedness. Halfway down, Rafael Point protrudes like a shark's tooth toward the southwest. This is one of the most exposed points along Vancouver Island's west coast, not an area to be trifled with. Here, shallow waters extend out to sea for a mile or more, encouraging the incoming swells to increase in size, or worse, to crest and break. From Crazy Eagle Beach to Cow Bay, the shoreline offers not a single place to land, nowhere to take respite from conditions that can degenerate in minutes.

There are those kayakers who have blithely travelled the outside of Flores with no concept of its danger because of their inexperience and their good fortune with the weather. Then there are those kayakers who began their journeys blithely, only to plunge into the realm of nightmares. On one expedition several kayakers capsized, and members of the group became separated from each other and lost in sudden fog. I cannot imagine the terror of being lost in fog on the outside of Flores. In fact, the risk of fog has consistently humbugged my efforts to take this dangerous route. Together with the threat of wind and unmanageable swell, the danger of fog and lack of a landing spot have thwarted my attempts to round Raphael Point on more occasions than they have allowed success. Two other factors can contribute to difficulties along this treacherous segment of the coast: seasickness and bursting bladders. As far as seasickness is concerned, kayakers are no less immune than any other group of ocean travellers, but since the physical weakness associated with nausea can be completely debilitating, seasickness is a serious risk in kayaking. Bladders, too, can be a definite problem after four hours in a wetsuit. In fact, the very act of pulling on a

Paddlers beware! The outer coast of Flores Island offers few escape routes. At times, the safest route lies miles from shore, away from the tumult of rocky shoals but prey to the perils of the open ocean.

146

wetsuit creates an almost immediate need to pee. I say "almost" because the impulse usually presents itself after launching, when land is a mile or two away.

We have not worn wetsuits on this trip. Instead, we have carefully assessed the daily risks posed by the route and weather conditions, and weighed them against our combined experience and safety equipment. Paddling the outer coast increases the level of risk, so an equal increase in precaution – such as a wetsuit – is appropriate.

Another precaution when paddling in dangerous areas is to choose companions whose level of ability and experience are of a known quantity and who are reliable in their reactions to situations. One of the most common errors of judgement in sea kayaking is made by stronger paddlers who leave the group behind without a care for the well being of those who may be struggling in their wake. The essence of good guiding is ensuring that the group stays together. To function as a unit, paddlers need to be within voice range of one another; otherwise, it is impossible to hear a cry for help. The more exposed the water, the more important it is to be within helping distance. On calm days a group can drift apart and still be within voice range. Windy days necessitate closer contact.

Underlying all of these notions is the importance of being completely honest and realistic about one's own personal skills and abilities and being aware of the extent of one's reliance on other people within the group. As with all activities that require physical tests of strength, kayaking has its fair share of those who consider themselves the strongest and therefore the most experienced. These people might naturally dominate a group and assume the role of the leader, but their leadership qualities might, in fact, be poor. Sadly, the truth of the matter is not always visible until after the fact. Sometimes the situations resulting from poor leadership are forgiving, almost benign. On the outer coast of Flores, there is no forgiveness; there is only luck. And the more time spent on the water, the more obvious it becomes that luck is finite.

Brand-new twin outboards roar to life as the *Matlahaw* pulls away from the dock. It feels strange to be sitting still as the scenery moves past, not moving my arms and swinging my upper body in the rhythmic cadence that is so satisfying, so hypnotic. The boat picks up speed as we leave the bay, slowing down only to negotiate the conditions at Sharp Point. Regardless of the size of the boat and the knowledge of the skipper, I am usually happiest in my own boat, under my own propulsion. Motorboats are finely designed; one small piece of broken metal and they will flounder helplessly, too big to be paddled or rowed, prey to the waves, the swell and the rocks. As we come around Sharp Point, I am relieved not to be dealing with the conditions, but glad that the kayaks are close by.

Once we reach calmer waters, the boat picks up speed and the land begins to blur. Places with which we have grown familiar flash by like postcards, now imbued with personal stories and memories. Places that I have yet to visit beckon alluringly. At one point we can see the entire length of Sydney Inlet. It is a spectacular example of a fjord, long and straight, the mountains slicing down precipitously to the water. Near the end of the inlet, the rounded shape of Sydney Cone pokes up conspicuously. It is said that prospective whalers would make a pilgrimage to the top of this mountain as part of their rigorous physical and spiritual training.

As we come through Hayden Passage, the swirling waters of an opposing tide have little impact on the speed of the boat. The constricted bottlenecks of Hayden and Sulphur Passages create strong tidal currents. If we were paddling right now we might be going backwards. It is more likely that we wouldn't have wasted the energy, and waited instead until slack tide.

Millar Channel is a dark blue, littered with whitecaps. We are heading into the wind now and the occasional wave splashes those of us who are sitting outside, at the back of the boat. But in minutes we reach the calm waters of Matilda Inlet, on our way to the dock at Ahousaht. The serene waters here conceal the wreck of the *Kingfisher*, a ship that was overpowered by the Ahousaht in 1864. After the crew of the *Kingfisher* had been killed, the vessel was burned and sunk, with rocks, to hide the attack from other ships.

Crowds of people are milling around the Ahousaht dock as we pull in. Even before the boat reaches the dock, some of the kids have recognized special faces. Their cries ring out: "Hi, Auntie!" "Hi, Grandma!" The woman next to me responds with obvious pride: "Hi, Grandson!" "Hi, Nephew!" As the kids rush to grab the tie-up lines, people quickly leave the boat – immediately caught up in the mêlée. No one else seems inclined to go to Tofino, so we leave without taking on extra passengers and head back down Matilda Inlet.

The conditions become progressively worse as we approach the open water between Flores and Vargas Islands. We have to move to the interior of the boat to avoid a constant soaking. Later, in the turbulent waters off Monks Rock, the situation deteriorates further, with waves swamping the boat entirely. I keep checking the kayaks, nervously anticipating a disaster of some variety. They are well tied on, however, and they are *boats*, after all; they are designed for getting wet.

Calmus Passage must have named by either a satirist or someone who chanced upon it on an exceptionally fine day. Whatever the case, the name in no way reflects the heaving chaos that we encounter. When we finally slide along the inner coast of Vargas, the water is calm, a pleasant change from the crashing and jarring. The boat accelerates, attempting to make up for the rough-water delay.

Suddenly an alarm sounds and the engines stop. Possibly there is something caught on the propellors, causing them to cavitate. The boat is thrown into reverse to dislodge whatever it is. We go forward again slowly, for a while, but soon the alarm shrills out again and the process is repeated. This pattern continues and our progression is of the stop-go-stop-go variety. The problem frustrates some, becomes a source of comic fodder for others. Inevitably the kayak jokes begin, with suggestions that these are at the heart of the problem and should be chucked overboard. I point out that if we're going to need a tow, it might be better to hang onto them. The verbal jousting continues good-naturedly as we hiccup along.

In a way, this group of people, in this situation, form a drop of the essence that embodies Clayoquot Sound: We are new residents and old residents; we are tourists and locals; we are held here by the land and the water, but for myriad reasons; our destination is still out of reach, but we have come through rough seas. If the need arises, we are capable of working together to get where we're going.

Clayoquot Sound has been the site of so much turbulence over the years, yet somehow its people have managed to emerge and continue. But the future of the sound is hazy at best, the visions of many people jostling for priority. Adding to the general mix of decision-making processes that exist here is the fact that Clayoquot Sound has applied to become a United Nations Biosphere Reserve. This is a broad designation that is supposed to facilitate conservation, while at the same time fostering certain types of economic growth that are considered appropriate and sustainable. The application has yet to be approved by the U.N. and has yet to gel into any sort of framework that will assist the residents of the sound on their journey into the future. For now we are all drifting in a metaphorical boat, advocating personal views while we trust in the future and hope for the best.

As we near Tofino, my own thoughts for the future are straightforward: unpack, clean up, repack and paddle back out. This desire to avoid reality is familiar; it grows with every wilderness adventure. The land and water fill me to the brim, catalysts for an internal element that simply cannot be ignited any other way. While I recognize that a swarm of mundane matters will doubtless press me sideways from my plans, it never hurts to aim high and keep the arrows handy.

From Tofino, Clayoquot Sound makes a stunning panorama. Without intimate exploration, however, it is just that – a view. This week Jan and Adrian and I became part of the panorama – immersed in the reality of the land and the water, the past and the present – each of us affected differently by those realities. Clayoquot Sound became three-dimensional for us, filling us with its omnipresence. Our journey may not have changed the view, but the contours are now aglow with personal associations.

In the concentric spiral of journeys, this has been one journey within many, or many journeys within one. It isn't until we have put away the boats and all the gear, however, that I retrieve the arrow of this particular expedition, taking its accumulated wealth of experiences with me and hoping to set it loose on other journeys soon.

The final stop: Tofino looms out of the fog. Reality gradually sinks in as the trip comes to a close. Now our focus will be on unpacking and cleaning up, and, of course, planning our next trip.

Afterword

TO TRAVEL SAFELY ON THE OCEAN IN A KAYAK REQUIRES A WEALTH OF EXPER-
ience. It is not the intent of this book to lay down instructions for kayaking, merely
to highlight some of the considerations involved. While the need for careful planning and good judgement cannot be overemphasized, respect for the power of the
sea is the foundation without which other skills cannot be built.

Travelling by kayak in Clayoquot Sound requires more than a knowledge of
paddling. It requires the strength and ability to handle severe weather; it requires an
understanding of tides and currents; it requires solid navigational skills; and it requires
a no-holds-barred assessment of yourself and your co-paddlers, of your individual
strengths and weaknesses. If the latter assessment leads you to conclude that perhaps
you are not up to such an expedition – then, bravo! If only others were so honest.

With a guide, however, it is possible for most novices to experience Clayoquot
Sound by kayak. A number of companies operate tours here. Pick up any sea kayaking magazine and there will doubtless be a smorgasbord of choices in it. To narrow
them down, choose a company that upholds the standards of either the Sea Kayak
Guides Alliance of B.C. or the Canadian Association of Sea Kayak Guides. To narrow
the field further, choose a company that has an obvious committment to the area
through which they travel, with guides whose experience of the area is extensive.

For a day trip into the sound from Tofino there are three local companies to
choose from: Tofino Sea Kayaking (250-725-4222), Remote Passages (250-725-3330)
and the Pacific Kayak Centre (250-725-3232). Of these, only Tofino Sea Kayaking
operates multiday tours and instructional courses. A new company, Rainforest Kayak
Adventures (1-877-422-WILD), plans to offer instructional trips.

For those who feel they are experienced enough to plan and execute their own trip, Tofino Sea Kayaking and the Pacific Kayak Centre offer rentals. Tofino Sea Kayaking also has their own paddling guide to Clayoquot Sound, which can assist in the planning of any trip. They have a variety of books on the area and sell the relevant charts: #3674 Clayoquot Sound (Northwest Portion) 1:40,000 and #3673 Clayoquot Sound (Southwest Portion) 1:40,000. These charts, and tide tables, are also available at the Tofino Co-op Hardware Store (250-725-3436) and Method Marine Ship's Chandlery (250-725-3251).

Should you decide to aim for Hotsprings Cove, there are a number of water taxis available, most of which are based out of Tofino. If you wish to support the locals of Hotsprings Cove, the most obvious choice is to use the *Matlahaw* (250-670-1106).

If you are paddling to Flores Island and want to book a guided tour on the Ahousaht Wild Side Heritage Trail, contact tour organizer Ramona Campbell (250-670-9586).

However you arrange to get out on the water, always file a route plan with friends. If you carry a marine VHF radio, channel 16 is designated for emergencies. Some cellphones work within range of Tofino, but are not yet an entirely reliable source of communication. Those relying on weather radios may wish to test them out first in Tofino, as reception in the sound is not always good. For those who are keen to harvest shellfish, contact the Department of Fisheries (250-725-3468) to check for red tide. B.C. Parks staff (250-726-2168) periodically cruise beaches within their designations in their boat, the *Clayoquot Ranger*, but so far there is no fee for recreational use of the beaches. In the future there may be fees for use, either in the parks or on Native land. The matters mentioned in this paragraph should be checked in Tofino before you leave on your trip.

Once your preparations are complete and you are launched, travel lightly on the land, leaving no trace of your presence. This means removing all garbage, including compost, defecating in low-tide areas where there is good water flow, burning all traces of toilet paper and resisting the temptation for large campfires. If you light a fire, use only small sticks and ensure that everything is burned to ashes.

Federal guidelines apply to the observation of whales and other marine mammals. The guidelines are available at most of the whale-watching outfits. Boats (including kayaks) are not allowed within 100 metres of a whale and should avoid crowding the animal against the shore. Observations at a distance of 100 metres should last only 30 minutes; after that period, observers must retreat to 300 metres. Kayaks are quiet craft; it is easy to surprise wildlife when you are in one of them. Avoid chasing animals and watch them calmly – from a distance, if possible.

As a final note, keep in mind that Clayoquot Sound is the traditional territory of the Tla-o-qui-aht, the Ahousaht and the Hesquiaht. Areas marked with I.R. (for "Indian Reservation") on the charts must be avoided. To show appreciation for having access to such a beautiful place, it would be respectful to contact the bands and ask for their sanction of your journey.